The Top Twelve

bestselling praise and worship anthems

ALL PRAISE RISING • BREATHE • FOREVER • HERE I AM TO WORSHIP
I NEED YOU MORE • LET EVERYTHING THAT HAS BREATH • SANCTUARY
STEP BY STEP • THE HEART OF WORSHIP • THE WONDERFUL CROSS
THERE IS JOY IN THE LORD • YOUR GRACE STILL AMAZES ME

lillenas.com

CONTENTS

June 27
8 & 9:30 services

Step by Step

with

O God, Our Help in Ages Past

Words and Music by
DAVID STRASSER
Arranged by Bruce Greer

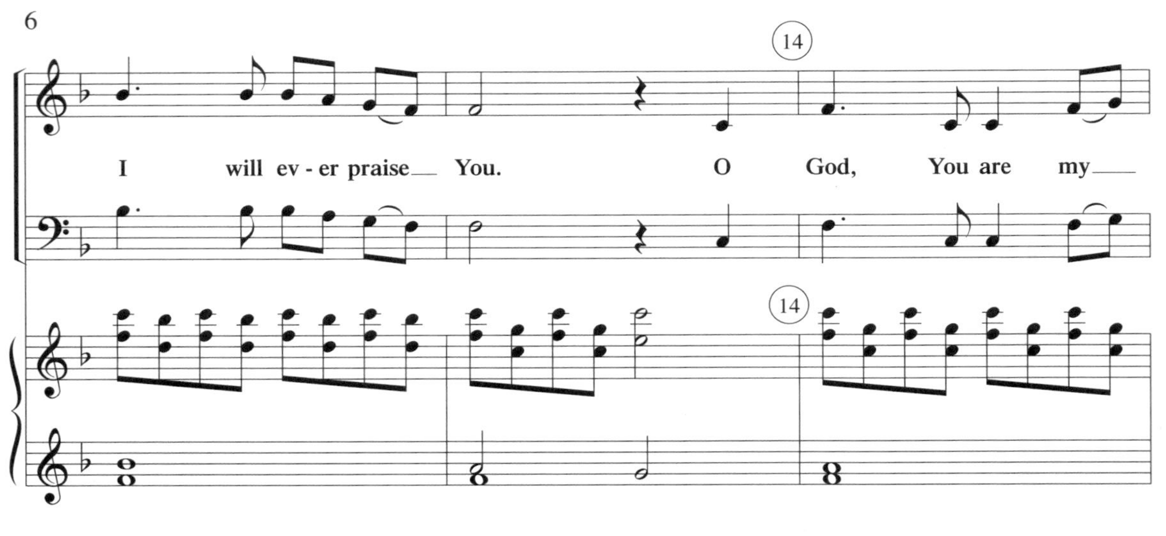
14
I will ev - er praise You. O God, You are my
14

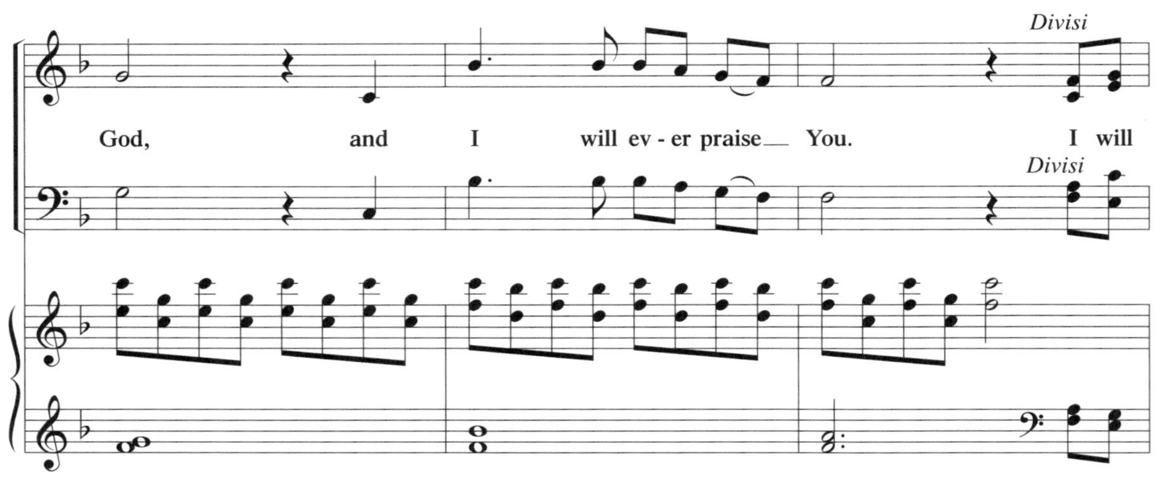
Divisi
God, and I will ev - er praise You. I will
Divisi

18
seek You in the morn - ing and I will learn to walk in Your
18
Dm7
F/C
C
B♭/D

*Words by ISAAC WATTS; Music by WILLIAM CROFT. Arr.

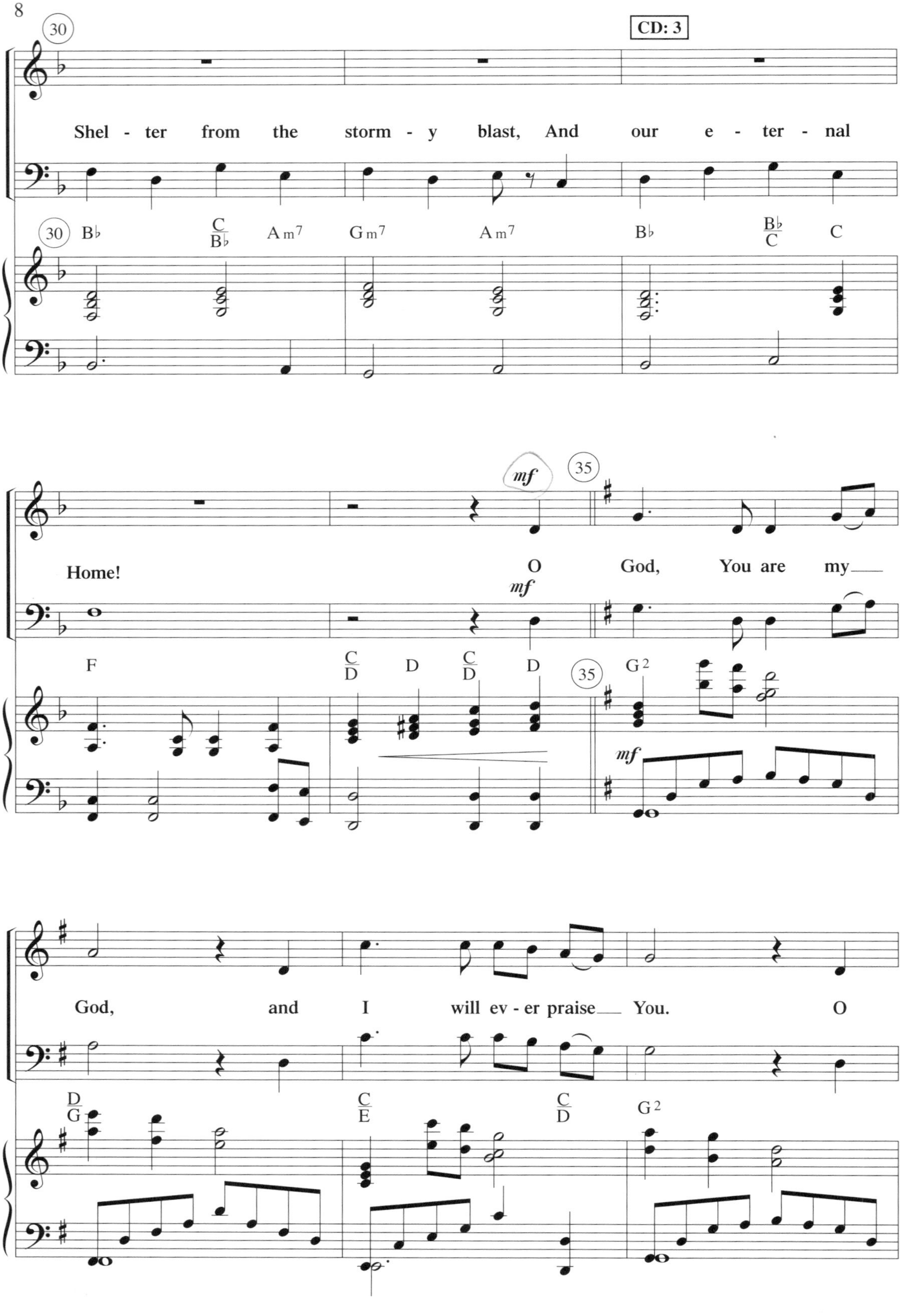

30 **CD: 3**

Shel - ter from the storm - y blast, And our e - ter - nal

30 B♭ C/B♭ Am7 Gm7 Am7 B♭ B♭/C C

Home! *mf* **O** 35 **God, You are my**

F C/D D C/D D 35 G2 *mf*

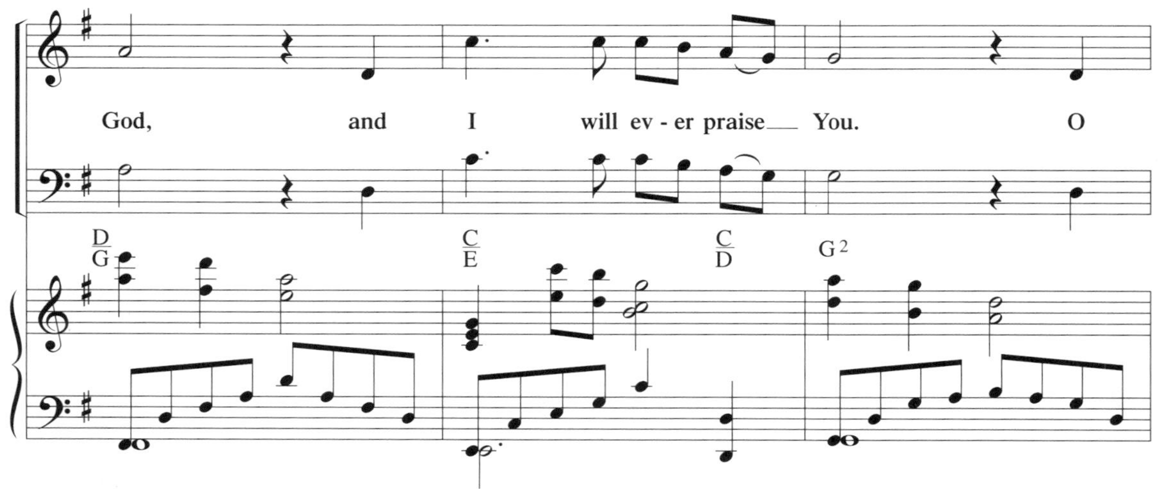

39
God, You are my God, and I will ev - er praise
G2
D
F♯
C
E
C
D
Divisi
43
You. I will seek You in the morn - ing and I will
Divisi
G2
Em
D
learn to walk in Your way; And step by step You'll lead
Unison
47
CD: 4
Unison
C
E
Am7
G2

50
— me
Un - der the shad - ow
and I will fol - low You all of my — days.
D2/F♯
C/E
C/D
N.C.
Divisi
of Thy throne Still may we dwell se - cure; Suf -
54
CD: 5
fi - cient — is Thine arm — a - lone, And our de - fense is

58
sure.
Be - fore the hills in or - der stood, Or
58
A♭2
B♭m7/A♭
62
earth re - ceived her frame, From ev - er - last - ing
Divisi
Fm7
B♭9
B♭m7/E♭
E♭
62
D♭/E♭
E♭
CD: 6
Thou art God, To end - less years the same. O
D♭/E♭
E♭
D♭/E♭
E♭
D♭/E♭
E♭

66
God, You are my God, and I will ev - er praise
A♭2
E♭2/G
D♭/F
D♭/E♭
70
You. O God, You are my God, and
A♭2
E♭2/G
Unison
74
I will ev - er praise You. I will seek You in the morn-
Unison
D♭/F
D♭/E♭
A♭2
Fm

- ing and I will learn to walk in Your way; And
E♭
D♭
B♭m7
D♭/E♭
78
Divisi
step by step You'll lead me and I will fol-low You all of my
Divisi
A♭2
E♭2/G
D♭/F
D♭/E♭
days.
82
N.C.

86 CD: 7

D♭/E♭ E♭ D♭/E♭ E♭ B♭m7 A♭2/C 86 D♭ Cm7

Watch

f

89 *Unison*

O God, our Help in

f *Unison*

F7sus F 89 B♭ E♭ B♭/D Gm

f

a - ges past, Our Hope for years to come, Be

E♭ F B♭ Gm Dm Gm/B♭ C F7sus F

CD: 8

93

Divisi

Thou our Guide while life shall last, And our e - ter - nal

Divisi

B♭ E♭ Cm F B♭/D E♭ D B♭ E♭ E♭/G Cm/E♭ B♭/E♭

93

97

Home. O God, You are my God, and

Cm7 F N.C. F/A

97

101

I will ev - er praise You. O God, You are my

E♭/G E♭/F B♭2 N.C.

101

Unison
God, and I will ev - er praise You. I will
Unison
F2/A
E♭/G
E♭/F
B♭2
105
seek You in the morn - ing and I will learn to walk in Your
105
Gm
F
E♭
109
Divisi
way; And step by step You'll lead me and I will
Divisi
Cm
E♭/F
109
N.C.
F2/A

CD: 9

fol - low You all of my ___ days. ___

E♭/G E♭/F N.C.

Unison 116

O God, our Help in

Unison

E♭/F F E♭/F F 116 Cm9 B♭2/D

a - ges past, Step by step You'll lead ___ us and we will

E♭2 B♭2/D Cm9 B♭2/D E♭2 Fsus

120
Divisi
ff
fol - low You,
O
Divisi
ff
Cm7
E♭
F
Cm7
F7sus
120

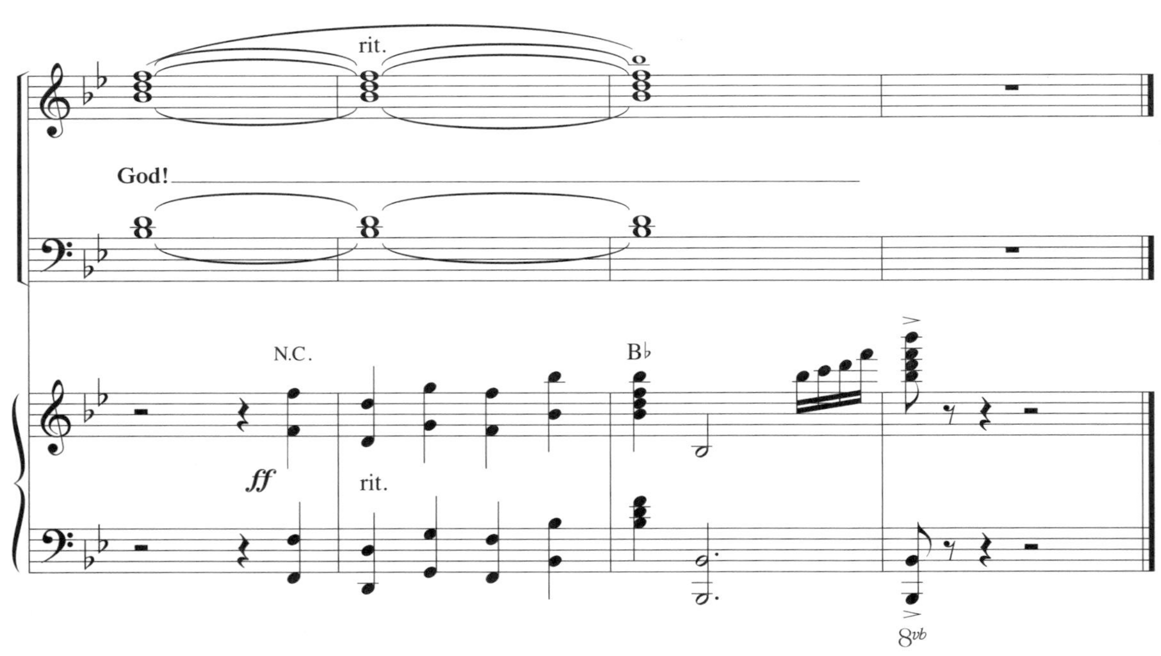
rit.
God!
N.C.
B♭
ff
rit.
8vb

Here I Am to Worship

Words and Music by
TIM HUGHES
Arranged by Russell Mauldin

11
Beau - ty that made this heart a - dore You,
E♭2
B♭2
Fm7
CD: 11
Hope of a life spent with You.
E♭2
B♭2
A♭2
mf
16
And here I am to wor - ship; here I am to
A♭2
E♭2
mf
bow down; Here I am to say that You're my God.
B♭/E♭
E♭/G

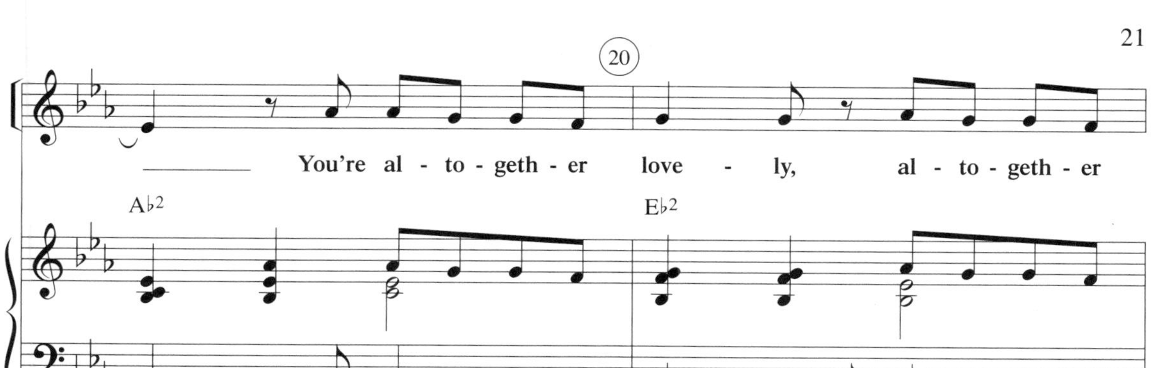
20
You're al - to - geth - er love - ly, al - to - geth - er
A♭2
E♭2

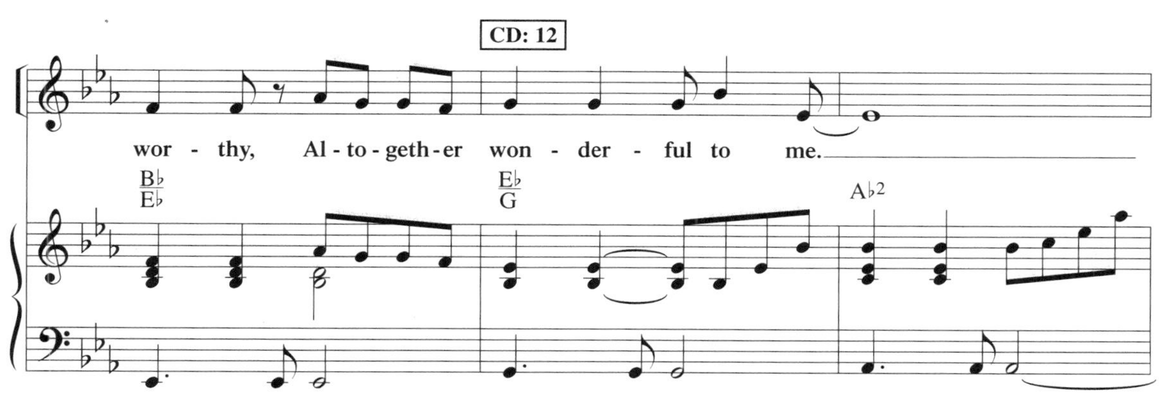
CD: 12
wor - thy, Al - to - geth - er won - der - ful to me.
B♭/E♭
E♭/G
A♭2

Choir
Unison
mf
25
King of all days, O so high - ly ex - alt - ed,
Unison
mf
A♭2
E♭2
B♭2
Fm7

Glo - rious in heav - en a - bove.
E♭2
B♭2
A♭2
29
Hum - bly You came to the earth You cre - at - ed,
E♭2
B♭2
Fm7
29
CD: 13
All for love's sake be - came poor.
E♭2
B♭2
A♭2

f
Divisi
34
And here I am to wor - ship; here I am to
f
Divisi
A♭2
34
E♭2
f
bow down; Here I am to say that You're my God.
B♭/D
E♭/G
38
You're al - to - geth - er love - ly, al - to - geth - er
A♭2
38
E♭2

CD: 14

wor - thy, Al - to - geth - er won - der - ful to me.
Unison
B♭/D
E♭/G
Unison
mf
42
And I'll nev - er know how much
A♭2
B♭
E♭/G
mf
it cost To see my sin up - on
A♭2
B♭
E♭/G

46
that cross.
And I'll nev - er know how much
mf
A♭2
46
B♭
E♭/G
CD: 15
it cost To see my sin up - on
A♭2
B♭
E♭/G
f
Divisi
50
that cross. No I'll nev - er know how much
f
Divisi
A♭2
50
B♭
E♭/G
f

it cost To see my sin up - on
A♭2
B♭
E♭/G
that cross. I'll nev - er know how
ff
54
CD: 16
much it cost.
decresc.

Unison
mp
58
Here I am to worship; here I am to
Unison
mp
A♭2
58
E♭2
mp
bow down; Here I am to say that You're my God.
B♭/D
E♭/G
62
You're al-to-geth-er love-ly, al-to-geth-er
A♭2
62
E♭2

CD: 17
wor - thy, Al - to - geth - er won - der - ful to me.
B♭
D
E♭
G
mf
Divisi
66
And here I am to wor - ship; here I am to
A♭2
E♭2
bow down; Here I am to say that You're my God.
B♭
D
E♭
G

70
You're al - to - geth - er love - ly, al - to - geth - er
A♭2
70
E♭2
CD: 18
wor - thy, Al - to - geth - er won - der - ful to me.
B♭/D
E♭/G
f
74
And here I am to wor - ship;
f
A♭2
74
E♭2
f

Unison
here I am to bow down;
Here I am to
Unison
B♭/D
E♭/G
A♭2
78
rit.
decresc.
mp
say that You're my God.
And here I am to
decresc.
mp
E♭/G
A♭2
A♭/B♭
rit.
decresc.
Divisi
wor - ship.
Divisi
E♭2
E♭
E♭2
mp

Forever

Words and Music by
CHRIS TOMLIN
Arranged by Michael Lawrence

God and King; His love en - dures for - ev - er.
G
15
For He is good He is a - bove all things; His love en - dures for - ev -
15
C2
Divisi mf
19
CD: 20
- er. Sing praise, sing
Divisi mf
G
19
D
mf

Unison
23
praise.
With a might - y hand and
C/E
23 G
out-stretched arm;
Divisi
His love en - dures for-ev - er.
G
27
Unison
For the life that's been re - born;
Divisi
His love en - dures for-ev -
27 C2

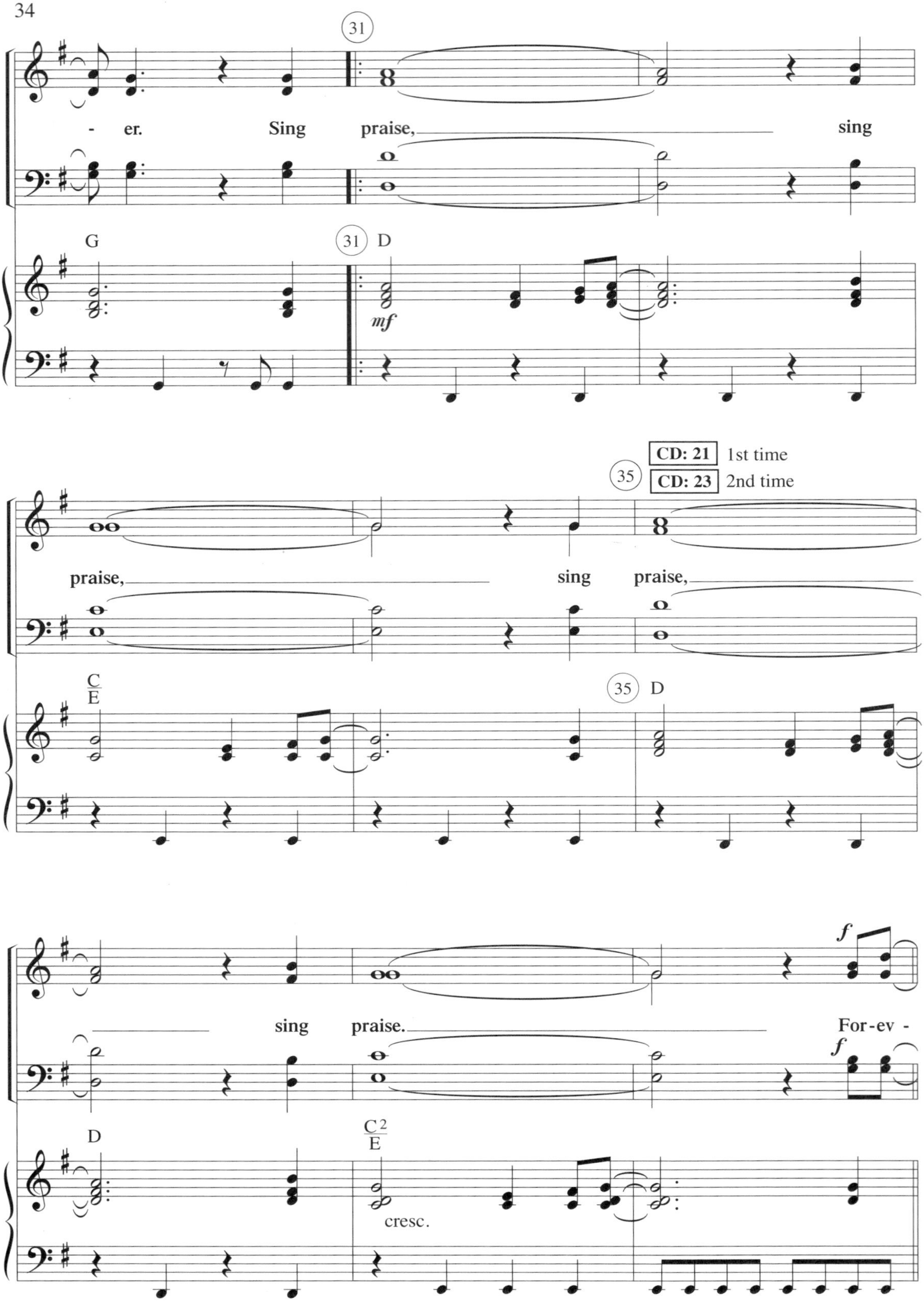

31

- er. Sing praise, sing

G 31 D

mf

CD: 21 1st time
35 CD: 23 2nd time

praise, sing praise,

C
E

35 D

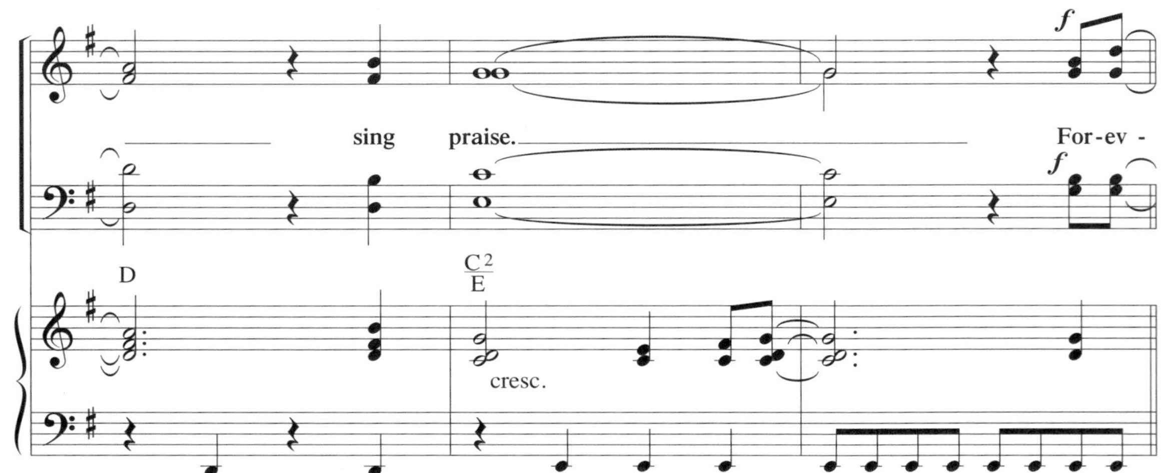

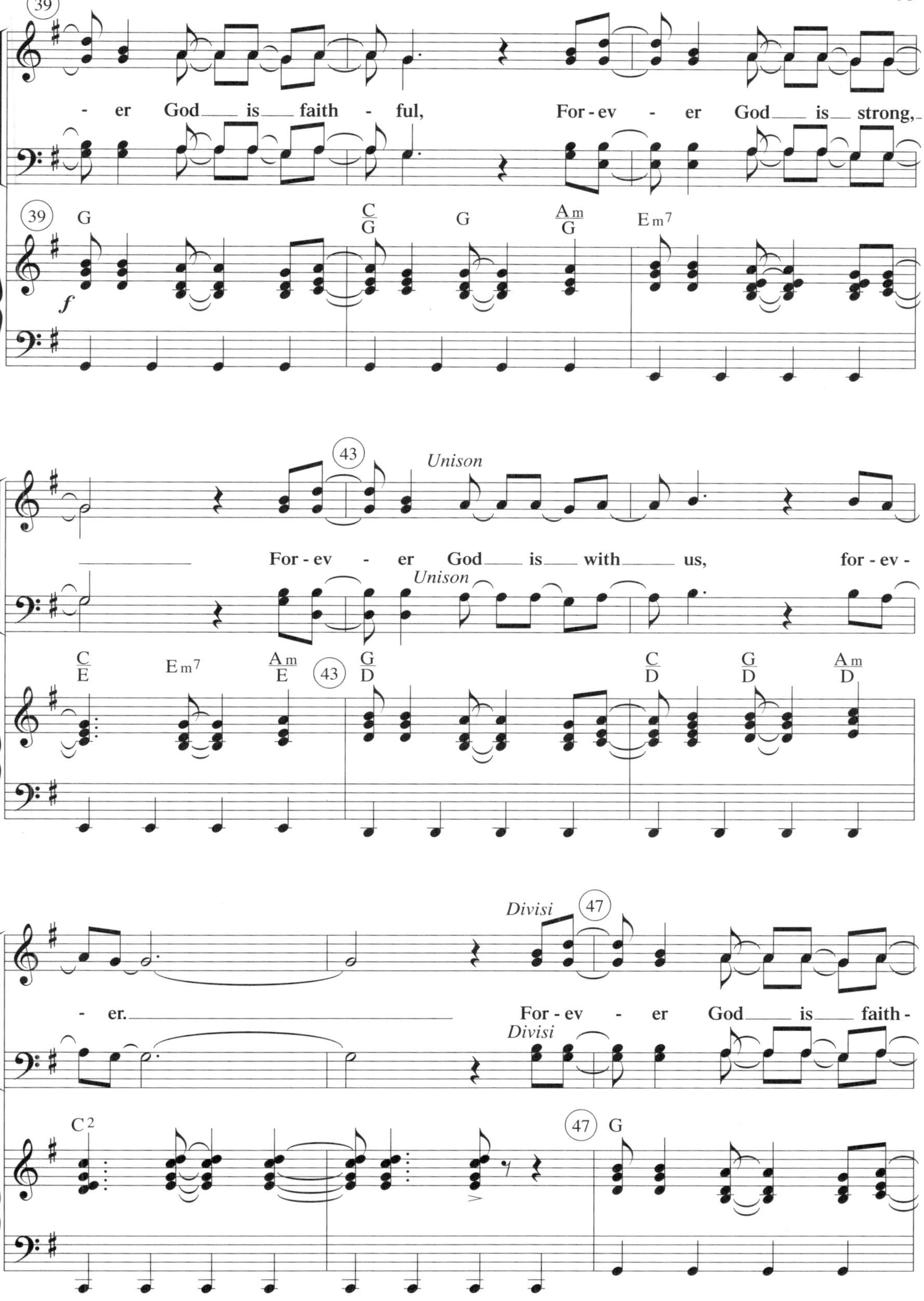
39
- er God is faith - ful, For - ev - er God is strong, -
39
G
C/G
G
Am/G
Em7
f
43
Unison
For - ev - er God is with us, for - ev -
Unison
C/E
Em7
Am/E
43
G/D
C/D
G/D
Am/D
Divisi
47
- er.
For - ev - er God is faith -
Divisi
C2
47
G

ful, For-ev - er God is strong, For-ev -
C/G G Am/G Em7 C/E Em7 Am/E
51
Unison
er God is with us, for-ev - er.
Unison
G/D C/D G/D Am/D C2
for-ev - er.
1 CD: 22
C2
1 G
mf

mp
59
From the ris - ing to the
G
59
mp
set - ting sun
Divisi
His love en - dures for - ev - er.
Unison
And by the
Divisi
G
63
grace of God we will car - ry on;
Divisi
His love en - dures for - ev -
63
C2

(to pg. 34, meas. 31)
2
mf
er.
Sing
er.
G
C/G
Am/G
69
CD: 24
Em7
C/E
Am/E
D sus
D
Divisi
73
For-ev - er God is faith - ful, For-ev-
D♭2/E♭
D♭M7/E♭
A♭
N.C.
Option: Perc. only

77

Unison

- er God __ is __ strong, __ For - ev - er God __ is __ with

Unison

77

__ us, for - ev - er. __ For - ev -

Divisi

Divisi

D♭2 D♭M9

81

- er God __ is __ faith - ful, For - ev - er God __ is __ strong, __

81

A♭ D♭/A♭ A♭ B♭m/A♭ Fm7

85
Unison
For - ev - er God is with us, for - ev -
Unison
D♭/F
Fm7
B♭m/F
85
A♭/E♭
D♭/E♭
A♭/E♭
B♭m/E♭
89
Divisi
- er.
For - ev - er God is faith-
Divisi
D♭2
89
A♭
- ful,
For - ev - er God is strong,
For - ev -
D♭/A♭
A♭
B♭m/A♭
Fm7
D♭/F
Fm7
B♭m/F

93
Unison
- er God is with us, for - ev - er.
Unison
A♭/E♭
D♭/E♭
A♭/E♭
B♭m/E♭
D♭2
93

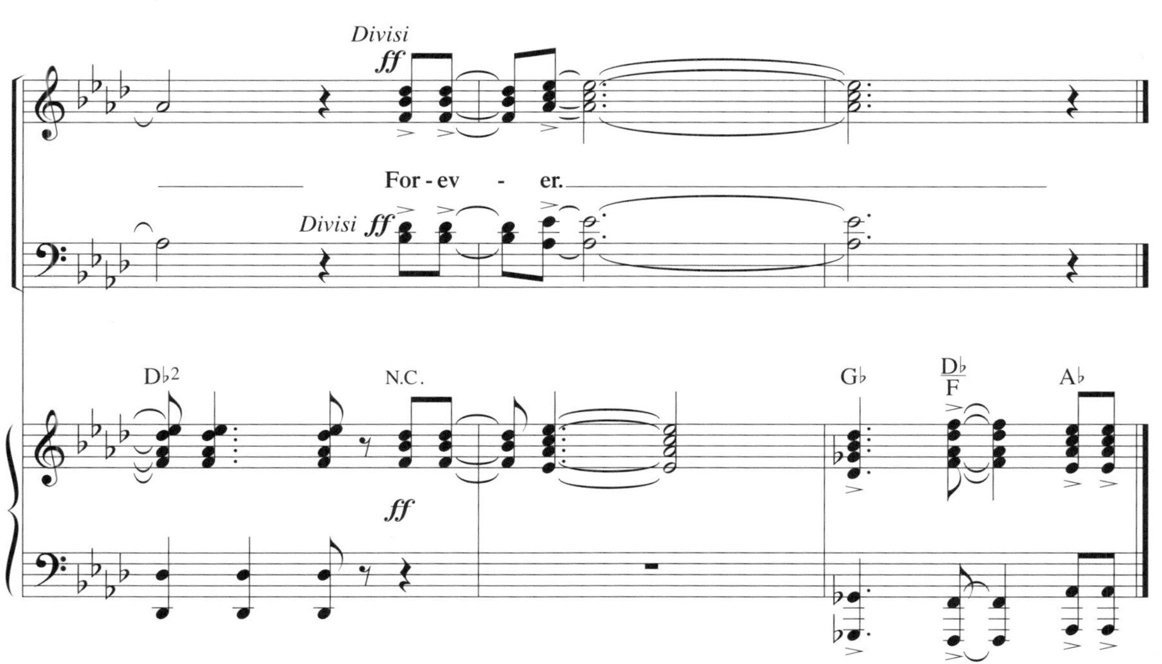
Divisi
ff
For - ev - er.
Divisi ff
D♭2
N.C.
G♭
D♭/F
A♭
ff

Breathe

Words and Music by
MARIE BARNETT
Arranged by Tom Fettke

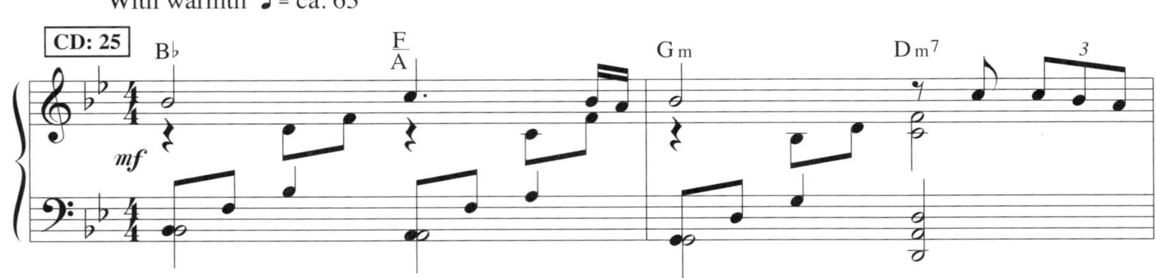

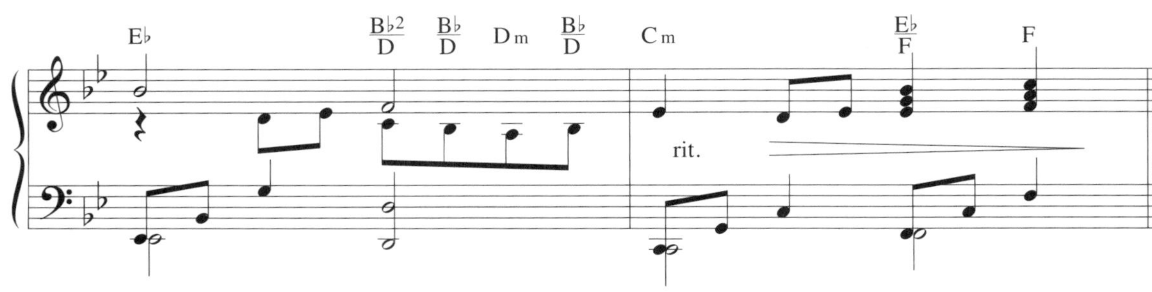

this is the air I breathe;
B♭
E♭2/B♭
9
Divisi
Your ho - ly pres - ence
Divisi
9
B♭
F/A
F/G
Gm
Gm/F
B♭M7/F
Unison
liv-ing in me.
13
This is my
Unison
E♭2
E♭
Gm
Gm7
Cm7/4
E♭2/F
F
13
B♭

dai - ly bread,
this is my
E♭2/B♭
B♭
dai-ly bread;
17
Divisi
Your ver - y Word
CD: 26
Divisi
E♭2/B♭
B♭
F/A
F/G
Gm
Gm/F
B♭M7/F
cresc.
spo - ken to me.
mf
And I'm,
E♭2
E♭
Gm
Gm7
Cm4 7
E♭2/F
F
cresc.

21
I'm des-p'rate for
21
B♭
F
A
Gm
Dm7
mf
You.
25
And I'm,
E♭
Gm
F
25
B♭
F
A
I'm lost with-out You.
Gm
Dm7
E♭
B♭
D

CD: 27
30
Unison
This is the
Unison
Cm7 Cm Gm/B♭ A♭M7 G7sus Gsus G
30
C2 C
air I breathe,
this is the
F2/C
C2 C
34
Divisi
air I breathe;
Your ho - ly
Divisi
F2/C
34
C G/B

Unison
pres - ence
liv - ing
in me.
Unison
G/A
Am
Am/G
Am9/G
F2
F
Am
Am7
G7sus/D
G7sus
G
38
This is my dai - ly bread,
38
C
F2/C
this is my dai - ly bread;
C
F2/C

42
CD: 28
Divisi
Your ver - y Word
Divisi
C
G
B
G
A
Am
Am
G
Am9
G
cresc.
spo - ken to me.
cresc.
And I'm,
f
F2
F
Am
Am7
Dm7
4
F2
G
G
cresc.
46
I'm des - p'rate for
3
C
G
B
Am
Em7
f

50
You.
And I'm,
F
Am
G
50
C
G
B
CD: 29
2nd time
1
(to pg. 48, meas. 46)
I'm lost with-out You.
And I'm,
3
Am
Em7
F
C
E
1
Dm7 4
F2
G
G
(to pg. 48, meas. 46)
2
55
decresc. poco a poco
I'm des-p'rate for You.
decresc. poco a poco
2
Dm7 4
G
Em7
55
F
Am
decresc. poco a poco

*For live worship, repeat as desired. Vamp is repeated once on the accompaniment tracks.

62
a tempo
Divisi
This is the air I breathe,
62
C
a tempo
F2
C
this is the air I breathe.
66
C
F2
C
66
C
rit.
F
C
C
C M7
F
C
rit.
C2
p

Your Grace Still Amazes Me

Words and Music by
SHAWN CRAIG and
CONNIE HARRINGTON
Arranged by Gaylen Bourland

With great emotion ♩ = ca. 60

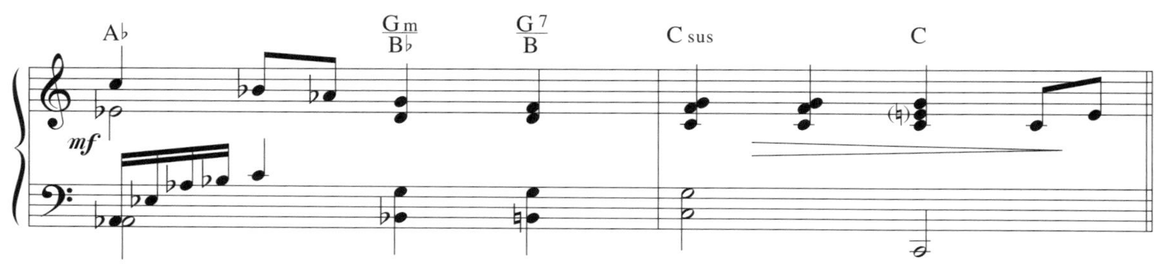

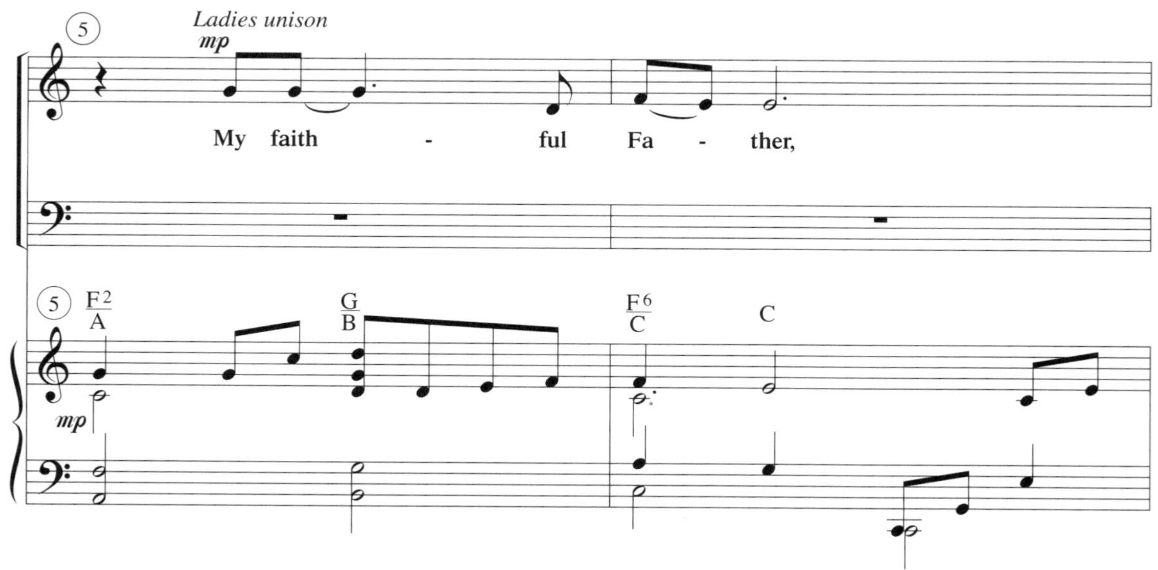

en - dur - ing Friend, Your ten - der mer -
F2/A G/B C2 C
9
- cy's like a riv - er with no end.
9 D7sus Dm7 Dm11 Dm11/C G2/B G/B F2/A F/A C/G
12
It o - ver - whelms me,
Men unison
mp
12 F2/A G/B F6/C C

cov - ers my sin. Each time I come
F2/A
G/B
C2
C
16
into Your presence I stand in won -
CD: 31
(,)
D7sus
Dm7
Dm11
Dm11/C
G2/B
G/B
C
Divisi
mf
- der once a - gain. Your grace
D7sus
Dm7
Gsus
G

20

still a - maz - es me, Your love

C C/E F Csus/F C2/E D7sus

is still a mys - ter - y; Each day

Gsus G2/B F/A G/B C F/C

24

I fall on my knees, be - cause Your

C C/E F E Am Am/G

CD: 34
2nd time
28
2nd time to Coda
(to pg. 60, meas. 50)
mp
grace still a - maz - es me, Your
mp
2nd time to Coda
(to pg. 60, meas. 50)
F
G sus
G
28
A m
A m/G
decresc.
grace still a - maz - es me.
F
G 4 2
G
F/A
G/B
mp
CD: 32
C
C/E
F
A♭
G m/B♭
G 7/B
C sus
C
mf

35

Solo
mp

O pa - tient Sav - ior,

Choir
Unison **mp**

Oo,

mp

35
F2/A G/B F6/C C

mp

You make me whole; You are the Au -

Divisi

F2/A G/B C2 C

39
- thor and the Heal - er of my soul.
39 D7sus Dm7 Dm11 Dm11/C G2/B G/B F2/A F/A C/G
43
What can I give You,
Unison
Oo,
F2/A G/B 43 F6/C C

what can I say? I know there's no
Divisi
F2/A
G/B
C2
C
cresc.
way to re - pay You, on - ly to of -
47
CD: 33
mf
Unison mf
On - ly to of -
Unison mf
D7sus
Dm7
Dm11
Dm11/C
G/B
C
cresc.

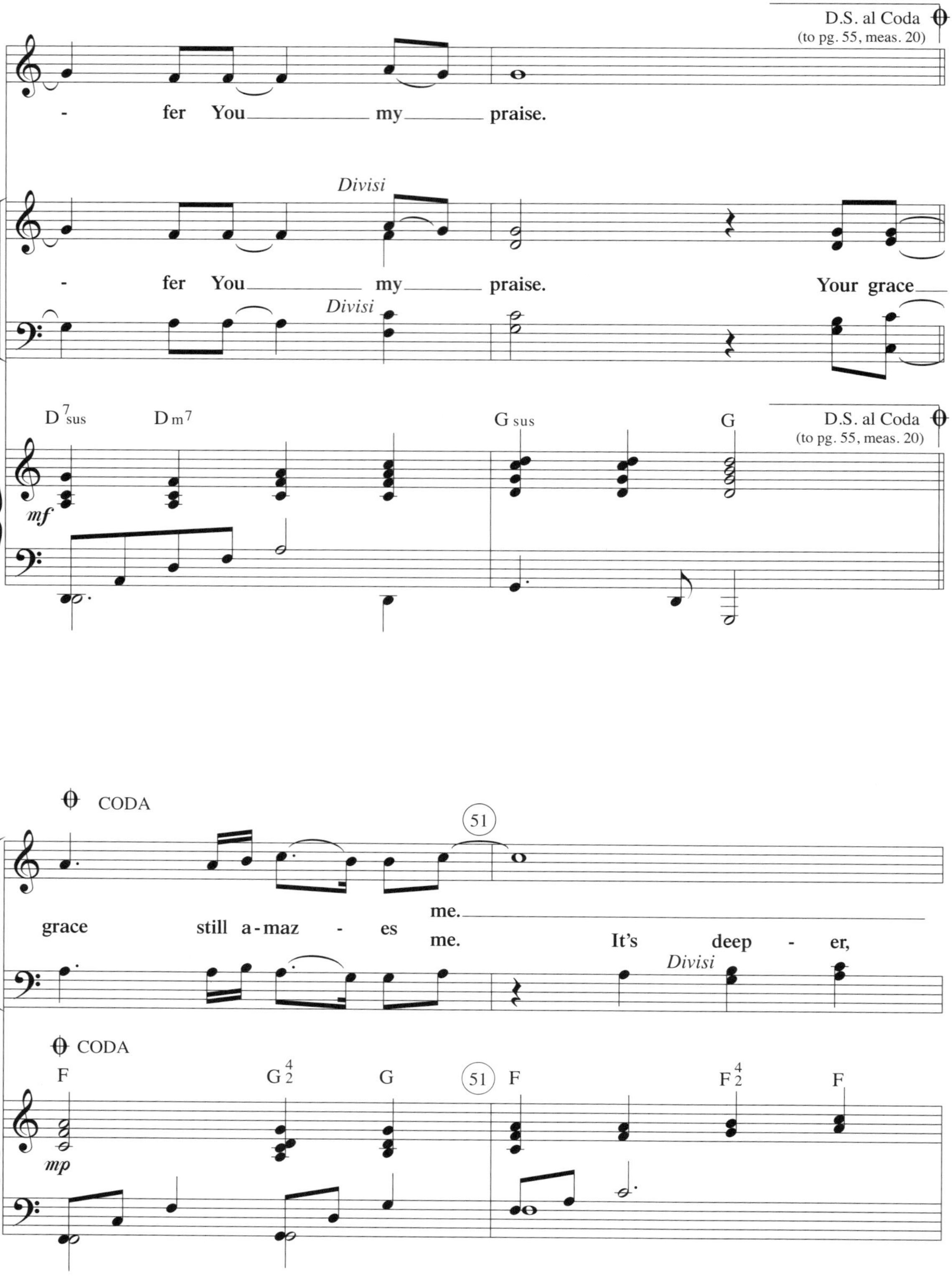

D.S. al Coda
(to pg. 55, meas. 20)

- fer You my praise.

Divisi

- fer You my praise. Your grace

Divisi

D7sus Dm7 Gsus G

D.S. al Coda
(to pg. 55, meas. 20)

mf

it's wid - er,
it's strong - er,
cresc.
Am/E
Am9/E
Am/E
F
F 4/2
F
cresc.
55
Divisi mf
It's
it's high - er,
It's deep - er,
mf
Am/E
Am9/E
Am/E
55
F
F 4/2
FM7
mf
deep - er,
it's
wid - er,
it's
it's wid - er,
it's strong - er,
D6/F♯
D7/F♯
D6/F♯
Am/F♯
CM9/G
C6/G
CM9/G
C/G

CD: 35
cresc.
strong - er,
it's high - er
than an - y - thing my
cresc.
D6/F♯ D9/F♯ D/F♯ C/G Dm/G F/G
cresc.
molto rit.
3
f
61
a tempo
Unison
eyes can see. Your grace still a -
Unison
C/G C4 2/G C/G Csus/G D♭/A♭ D♭
molto rit.
f a tempo
maz - es me, Your love is still a
G♭ D♭sus/G♭ D♭2/F E♭m7 A♭sus A♭2/C

65
Divisi
mys - ter - y; Each day I fall on my
Divisi
G♭/B♭ A♭/C D♭ G♭/D♭ D♭ D♭/F G♭ F
65
knees, be - cause Your grace still a-maz - es me,
B♭m B♭m/A♭ G♭ A♭sus A♭
69
decresc.
mp
Your
decresc.
mp
B♭m B♭m/A♭
69
decresc.

grace still a-maz - es me.
G♭
A♭ 4 2
A♭
G♭ B♭
mp
A♭ C
D♭
D♭ F
G♭
75
A
A♭m C♭
A♭7 C
rit.
p
A - maz - ing grace.
(6)
D♭sus
D♭
G♭ A♭
G♭m A♭
D♭

Let Everything That Has Breath

Words and Music by
MATT REDMAN
Arranged by Richard Kingsmore

Driving ♩ = ca. 120

CD: 36

D2 | A/D | G2/D | A/D | 5 D2 | A/C♯ | Bm7 | G2 | Em7/4

mf

1st time: Choir unison
2nd time: Choir parts

10

f

Let ev - 'ry - thing ___ that, ev - 'ry - thing ___ that,

10 D2 | A/C♯

f

ev - 'ry - thing that has breath praise the Lord.
B m7
E m / G
D / G
14
Ev - 'ry - thing that, ev - 'ry - thing that,
14
D 2
A / C♯
CD: 37 1st time
CD: 39 2nd time
ev - 'ry - thing that has breath praise the Lord.
B m7
E m / G
D / G

Em7/4
20
Solo
mf
1. Praise You in the morn-ing,
2. Praise You in the heav-ens,
praise You in the ev - 'ning,
join - ing with the an - gels,
D(no 3)
A
mf
praise You when I'm young and when I'm old.
prais - ing You for - ev - er and a day.
Bm
G2(no 3)

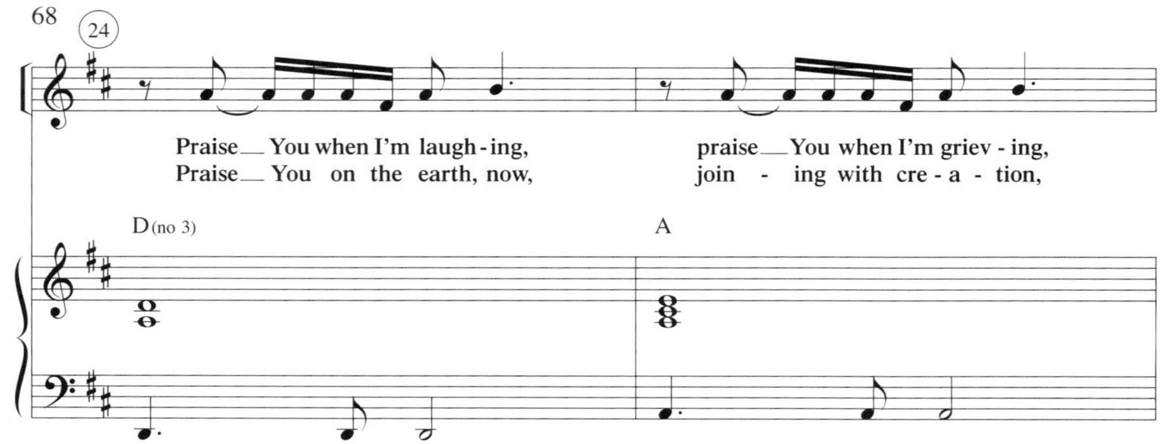
24
Praise — You when I'm laugh - ing,
Praise — You on the earth, now,
praise — You when I'm griev - ing,
join - ing with cre - a - tion,
D(no 3)
A

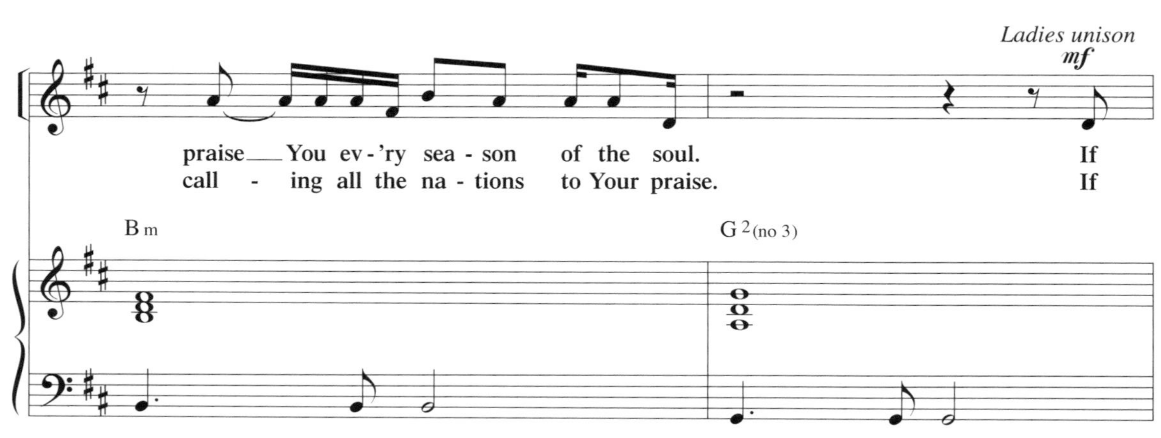
Ladies unison
mf
praise — You ev - 'ry sea - son of the soul.
call - ing all the na - tions to Your praise.
If
If
Bm
G2(no 3)

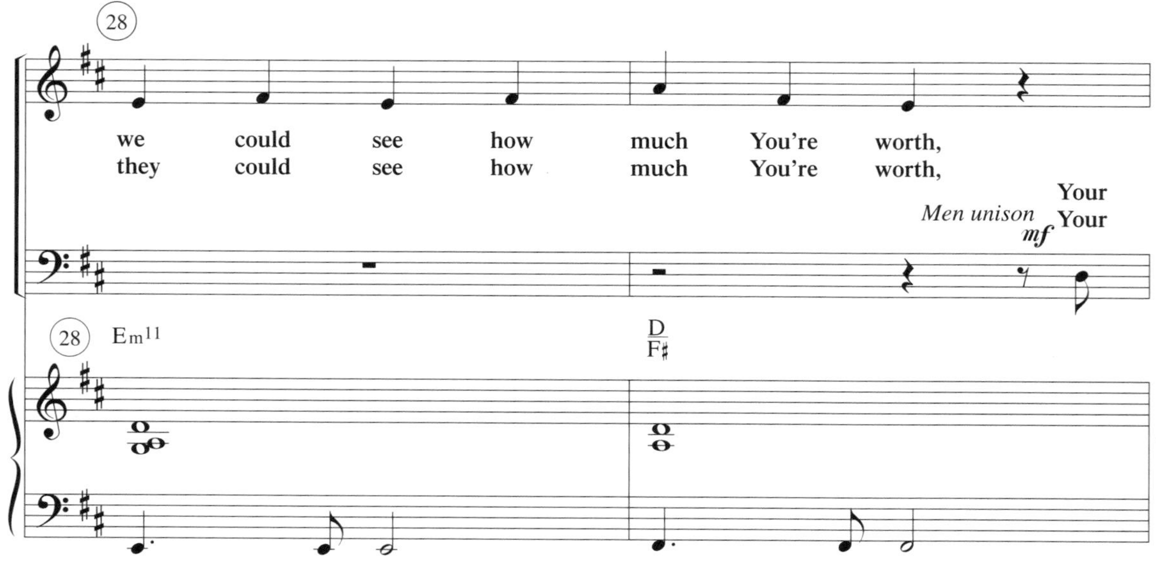
28
we could see how much You're worth,
they could see how much You're worth,
Men unison
mf
Your
Your
Em11
D/F♯

Then
Then
pow'r, Your might, Your end - less love,
pow'r, Your might, Your end - less love,
Em11
D
F♯
CD: 38 1st time
CD: 40 2nd time
32
sure - ly we would nev - er cease to
sure - ly they would nev - er cease to
32
Em11
D
F♯
1
(to pg. 65, meas. 10)
praise
praise
You!
G2
1
(to pg. 65, meas. 10)
A sus
A

2
cresc.
You!
cresc.
37
f
Divisi
Let ev - 'ry - thing that,
Divisi f
2
A sus
B♭sus
B♭
37
E♭2
f
ev - 'ry - thing that,
ev - 'ry - thing that
B♭/D
C m7
41
has breath praise the Lord.
Ev - 'ry - thing that,
Fm/A♭
E♭/A♭
41
E♭2

ev - 'ry - thing that, ev - 'ry - thing that
B♭/D
Cm7
has breath praise the Lord.
Unison
45
Fm/A♭
E♭/A♭
E♭2
3
CD: 41
Fm7
A♭/D♭
E♭/A♭
Fm7
E♭sus/D♭
Fsus/C

49
Divisi
Let ev - 'ry - thing that,
F sus
C
F2
ev - 'ry - thing that,
ev - 'ry - thing that
C
E
D m7
has breath praise the Lord.
53
Ev - 'ry - thing that,
G m
B♭
F
B♭

CD: 42
1st time
ev - 'ry - thing that,
ev - 'ry - thing that
C/E
Dm7
1
(to pg. 72, meas. 49)
2
has breath praise the Lord.
has breath praise the Lord.
1
Gm/B♭
F/B♭
(to pg. 72, meas. 49)
2
Gm/B♭
F/B♭
F2
C/F

60
Ev - 'ry - thing that has breath praise the Lord!
60
B♭2/F
B♭/C
C
64
Ev - 'ry - thing that
F2
C/F
64
B♭2/F
(8)
has breath praise the Lord!
B♭/C
C
F

The Wonderful Cross

ISAAC WATTS, CHRIS TOMLIN,
JESSE REEVES and J. D. WALT

LOWELL MASON, CHRIS TOMLIN,
JESSE REEVES and J. D. WALT
Arranged by Camp Kirkland

vey the won - drous cross
head, His hands, His feet,
C2
Fm6/C
C2
13
On which the Prince of Glo - ry
Sor - row and love flow min - gled
13
C2
Fm6/C
C2
died, My rich - est gain I
down. Did e'er such love and
17
Fm6/C
17
C2

21
count but loss, And pour con -
sor - row meet, Or thorns com -
Fm6/C
C2
21
CD: 45
2nd time
1
tempt on all my pride.
pose so rich a
E7/G♯
Am
Fm6
C2
CD: 44
(to pg. 75, meas. 9)
2
cresc.
crown?
cresc.
Fsus/C
Fm6/C
(to pg. 75, meas. 9)
2
C2
cresc.

Divisi
f
30
O the won - der - ful cross, O the
f Divisi
C2
C
C/E
G/F
F2
C2/E
f
wonder - ful cross
Unison
34
Bids me come and die, and find
Unison
G/F
F2
C2/E
F2
that I may tru - ly live.
Divisi
O the
Divisi
C2/E
G sus
G
C/E

38
Unison
won - der - ful cross,
O the won - der - ful cross;
G/F
F2
C2/E
All who gath - er here by grace draw near and bless
Unison
42
CD: 46
decresc.
Your name.
46
mp
3. Were the whole
G sus
G
C2

realm of na - ture mine,
C2
Fm6/C
C2
50
CD: 47
That were a pres - ent far too
50
C2
Fm6/C
C2
small.
54
mf
Love so a - maz - ing,
mf
Fm6/C
54
D♭2
mf

58
f
so di - vine, De - mands my
Gbm6
Db
Db2
Gb2
Bb
cresc.
CD: 48
Divisi
soul, my life, my all!
Db
Ab
Gb
Ab
Db
63
O the won - der - ful cross, O the
Db
F
Ab
Gb
Gb2
Db2
F

Unison
67
won - der - ful cross Bids me come and die, and find
Unison
A♭/G♭
G♭2
D♭2/F
67
G♭2
Divisi
that I may tru - ly live.
O the
Divisi
D♭2/F
A♭sus
A♭
D♭/F
71
won - der - ful cross, O the won - der - ful cross;
Unison
71
A♭/G♭
G♭2
D♭2/F
A♭/G♭
G♭2

75
All who gath - er here by grace draw near and bless
Unison
D♭2
F
G♭2
D♭2
F
Your name.
CD: 49
A♭sus
A♭
G♭2
B♭
mf
A♭sus
A
81
mf
Love so a - maz - ing, so di -
mf
D♭2
G♭m6
D♭

85
vine, De - mands my soul, my
D♭2
85
G♭m6
D♭
life, my all!
mp
mp
D♭2
mp
91
My soul, my
8va
D♭2
91
G♭m6
D♭
8va

95
all!
My
life,
D♭2
8va
Gbm6
D♭
my
all!
D♭2

The Heart of Worship

Words and Music by
MATT REDMAN
Arranged by Marty Parks

Reverently ♩ = ca. 74

CD: 50

N.C.

mp

6

Ladies unison

mp

When the mu - sic fades, all is stripped a - way, and I sim - ply come;

(10)

Long-ing just to bring something that's of worth

Long-ing just to bring,

Men unison *mp*

(10) E♭2 — B♭/E♭

CD: 51

that will bless Your heart;

that will bless Your heart;

Fm4/E♭ — B♭sus — B♭

(14) 𝄋 *Choir* *mf*

I'll bring You more than a song, for a song in it - self

mf More than a song; in it - self

(14) 𝄋 Fm7 — E♭2/G — E♭/G — B♭sus — B♭ — E♭/B♭

mf

is not what You have re - quired.
is not what You have re - quired.
Fm7
E♭2/G
E♭/G
B♭sus
B♭
18
You search much deep - er with - in thro' the way things ap - pear;
Deep - er with - in; things ap - pear;
CD: 52 1st time
CD: 55 2nd time
Divisi
You're look - ing in - to my heart.
You're look - ing in - to my heart.
A♭
E♭/B♭

22
I'm com - ing back to the heart of wor - ship, And it's
Divisi
22
E♭
B♭2/D
B♭/D
all a - bout You; all a - bout You, Je - sus.
Fm9
A♭M7
B♭6
B♭7
26
I'm sor - ry, Lord, for the thing I've made it, When it's
26
E♭
B♭2/D
B♭/D

CD: 56
2nd time
2nd time to Coda
(to pg. 91, meas. 42)
30
all a-bout You;
all a-bout You, Je - sus.
Fm9
A♭M7
B♭6
B♭7
E♭
CD: 53
C♭
D♭
E♭4/2
E♭
Fm7/B♭
f
34
Praise Team (or 3-part choir)
mf
King of end - less worth,
no one could ex-press
B♭/E♭

how much You de - serve.
A♭/E♭
B♭sus
B♭
38
Tho' I'm weak and poor,
all I have is Yours,
38
E♭
B♭/E♭
CD: 54
D.S. al Coda
(to pg. 87, meas. 14)
CODA
ev-'ry sin-gle breath.
all a-bout You.
D.S. al Coda
(to pg. 87, meas. 14)
CODA
A♭/E♭
B♭sus
B♭
A♭M7
B♭sus
C sus
C

43

Praise Team

f

I'm back to the heart of wor - ship;

Choir

f

I'm coming back to the heart of wor - ship, And it's

f

43

F C2/E C/E

f

All a - bout You, Je - sus.

all a - bout You; all a - bout You, Je - sus.

Gm9 B♭M7 C6 C7

47
O Lord, for the thing I've made it;
I'm sor - ry, Lord, for the thing I've made it, When it's
F
C2/E
C/E
47
All a - bout You, Je - sus.
1
(to pg. 92, meas. 43)
all a - bout You; all a - bout You, Je - sus.
Gm9
B♭M7
C6
C7
1
(to pg. 92, meas. 43)

2
52
Je - sus!
all a-bout You, Je - sus!
2
B♭M7
C6
C7
F
C
E
CD: 57
56
mf
To the heart
Unison mf
I'm com-ing back.
Unison mf
Dm
C7sus
F
Gm
F
mf

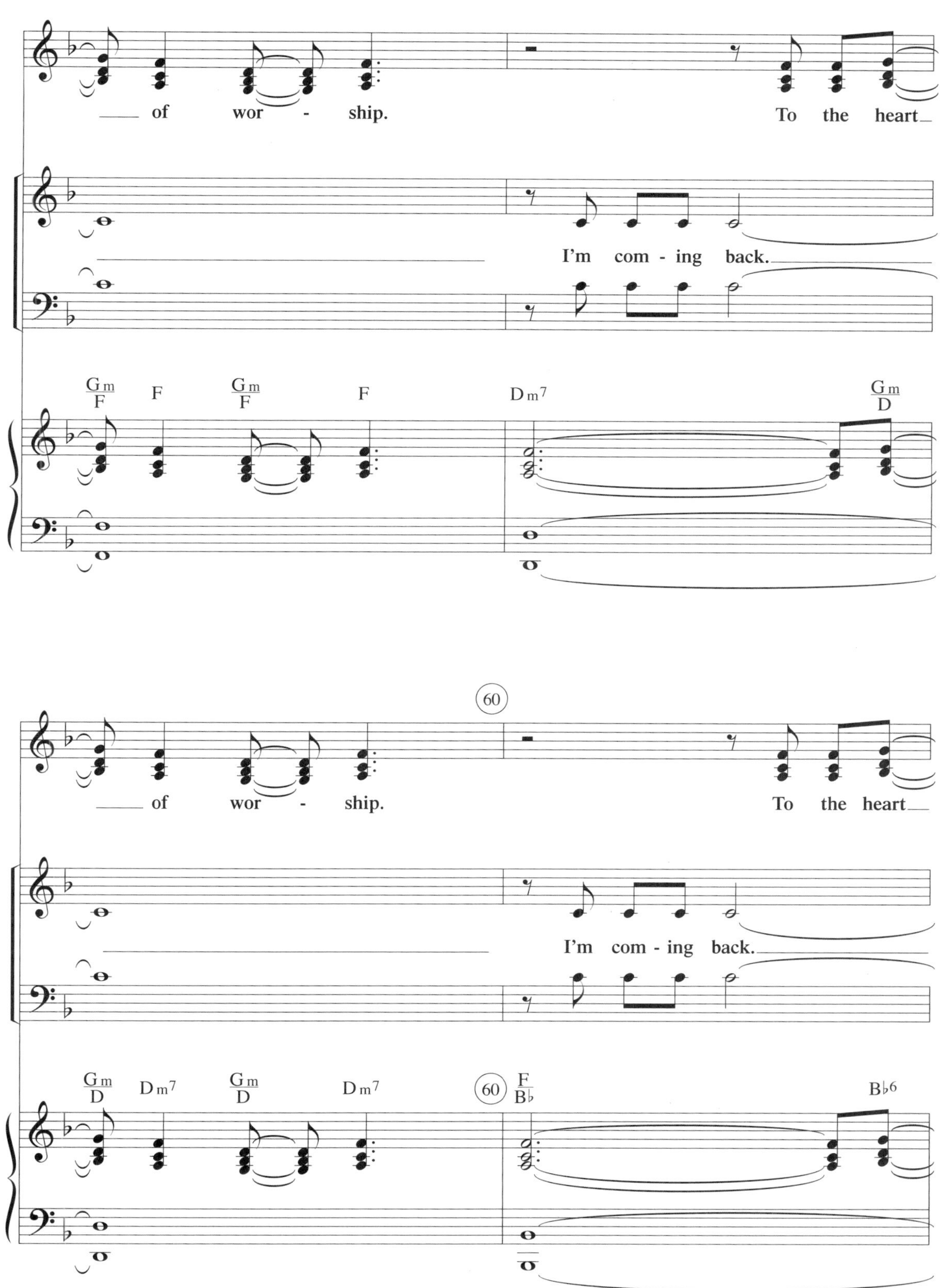
of wor - ship.
To the heart
I'm com - ing back.
Gm/F
F
Gm/F
F
Dm7
Gm/D
60
of wor - ship.
To the heart
I'm com - ing back.
Gm/D
Dm7
Gm/D
Dm7
60
F/B♭
B♭6

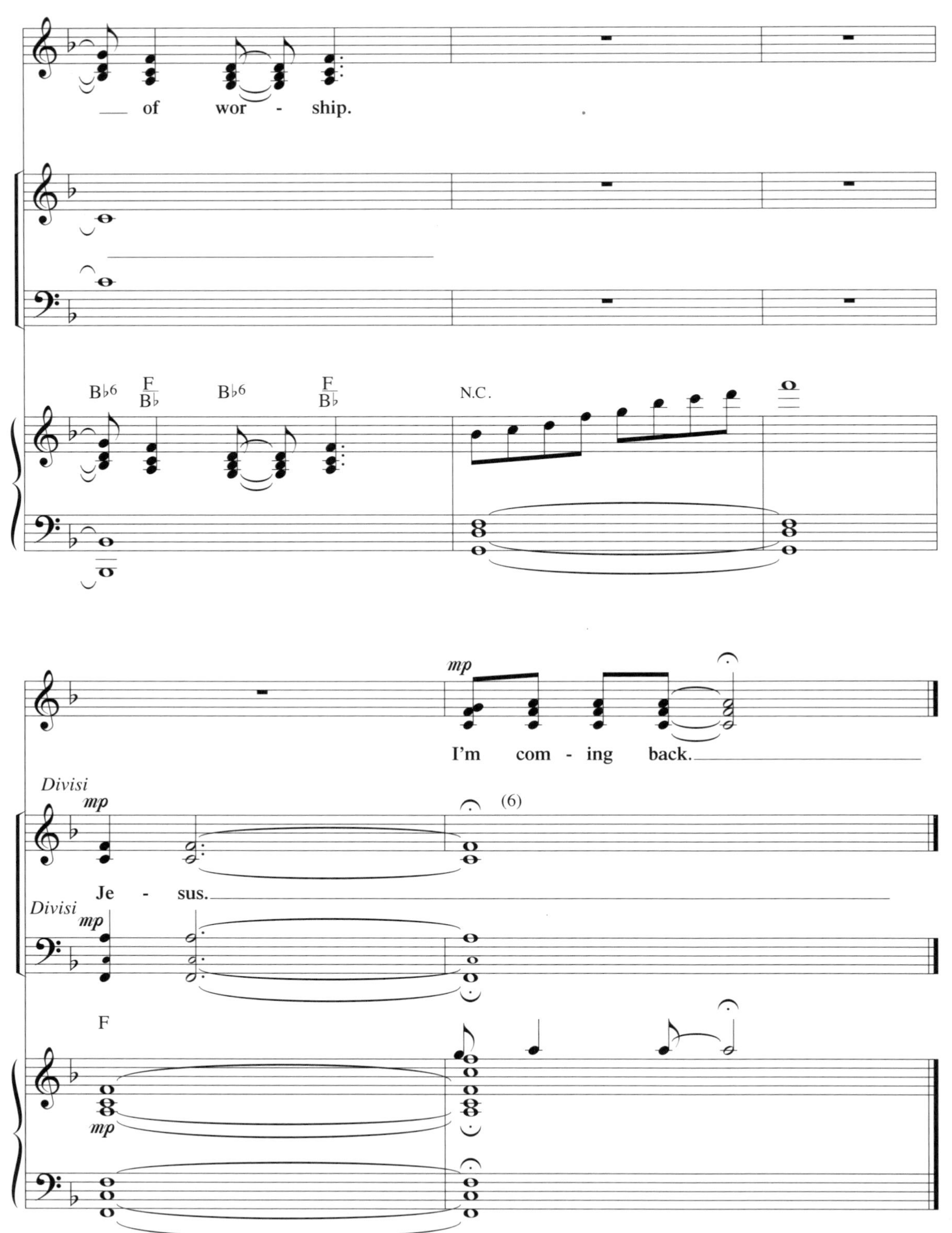
of wor - ship.
B♭6
F/B♭
B♭6
F/B♭
N.C.
mp
I'm com - ing back.
Divisi
mp
(6)
Je - sus.
Divisi
mp
F
mp

Sanctuary

with

Take My Life, and Let It Be Consecrated

Words and Music by
JOHN W. THOMPSON
and RANDY SCRUGGS
Arranged by Bruce Greer

Start here
9
CD: 59
giv - ing, I'll be a liv - ing sanc-tu - ar - y for
You.
Divisi mp
13
Lord, pre - pare me to be a sanc-tu - ar - y,
Divisi mp
13
mp
Pure and ho - ly, tried and true. With thanks-

*Words by FRANCES R. HAVERGAL; Music by HENRI A. CESAR MALAN. Arr.

28
Con - se - crat - ed, Lord, to Thee.
Take my mo - ments
Cm7 E♭/A♭ Fm7 E♭/B♭ B♭ E♭ F/E♭
and my days,
CD: 61
Let them flow in cease - less praise;
A♭m/E♭ E♭sus E♭ E♭/G A♭ E♭/G B♭7/F E♭4/2 E♭ E♭/B♭ B♭
mp
Divisi
34
Let them flow in cease - less praise. Lord, pre - pare me
Cm B♭ A♭M7 Fm7 E♭/B♭ B♭ E♭ Gm/B♭ Fm/B♭ E♭

to be a sanc - tu - ar - y, Pure and ho - ly, tried and
E♭
B♭2/D
A♭2/C
38
true. With thanks - giv - ing, I'll be a liv - ing sanc - tu -
E♭/B♭
B♭
Gm/B♭
Fm/B♭
E♭
B♭2/D
mf
CD: 62
42
Unison
ar - y for You.
Take my love, my
A♭2/C
B♭/C
C
F
Dm7

Lord, I pour At Thy feet its treasure store.
Gm4 7 Bb/C F Dm7 F/Bb Gm7 F/C C F
46 Divisi
Take my-self and I will be Ever, only,
Divisi
F G/F Bbm/F Fsus F F/A Bb F/A
46
all for Thee,
50 Unison
Ever, only, all for Thee.
CD: 63
Unison
C7/G F4 2 F F/C C Dm C BbM7 Gm7 F/C C F
50

53
f
Take my will and make it Thine,
C/D D C/D D G N.C.
57 Divisi
It shall be no long - er mine. Take my heart– it
G A/G
is Thine own; It shall be Thy roy - al throne;
CD: 64
Cm/G Gsus G G/B C G/B D7/A G4/2 G G/D D

Unison
Divisi
63
It shall be Thy roy - al throne. Lord, pre - pare me
Em D CM7 Am7 G/D D G Bm/D Am/D G
to be a sanc-tu - ar - y, Pure and ho - ly, tried and
G D2/F♯ C2/E
true. With thanks-giv - ing, I'll be a liv - ing sanc-tu -
67
G/D D Bm/D Am/D G D2/F♯

CD: 65
rit.
Choir only
ff
ar - y for You.
throne
Lord, pre -
C2/E
Bm/D Am/D
G
E♭M7/F
Fsus
E♭M7/F
F
cresc.
rit.
72
Broader tempo ♩ = ca. 69
pare me to be a sanc-tu - ar - y, Pure and ho - ly,
B♭
ff Broader
F2/A
E♭2/G
tried and true. With thanks-giv - ing, I'll be a
76
E♭2/G
B♭/F
F
Dm/F Cm/F
B♭

Decresc.
PRAYERF
living sanctuary for You. With thanks-
F2/A
E♭2/G
Dm/F Cm/F
Gm
B♭M7/F
E♭
Dm/F Cm/F
80
giving, I'll be a living sanctu-
B♭
F2/A
rit.
Unison
ary for You.
Unison
E♭2/G
Dm/F Cm/F
B♭2
N.C.

85
CD: 66
Cm7
B♭2
D
E♭2
decresc.
mp
89
With thanks - giv - ing, I'll be a liv - ing sanc-tu -
B♭
F
A
rit.
Divisi
p
for You.
(6)
ar - y Lord, for You.
Divisi p
B♭2

There Is Joy in the Lord

Words and Music by
CHERI KEAGGY
Arranged by Richard Kingsmore

13
hope in the know - ledge of Him.
E♭
B♭
B♭sus
B♭
A♭

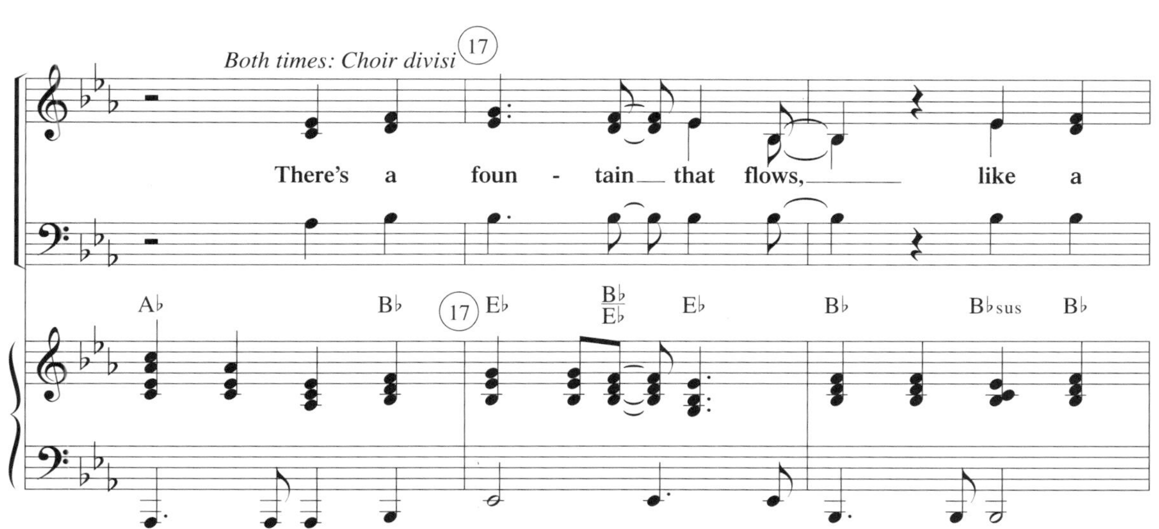
Both times: Choir divisi
17
There's a foun - tain that flows, like a
A♭
B♭
17
E♭
B♭/E♭
E♭
B♭
B♭sus
B♭

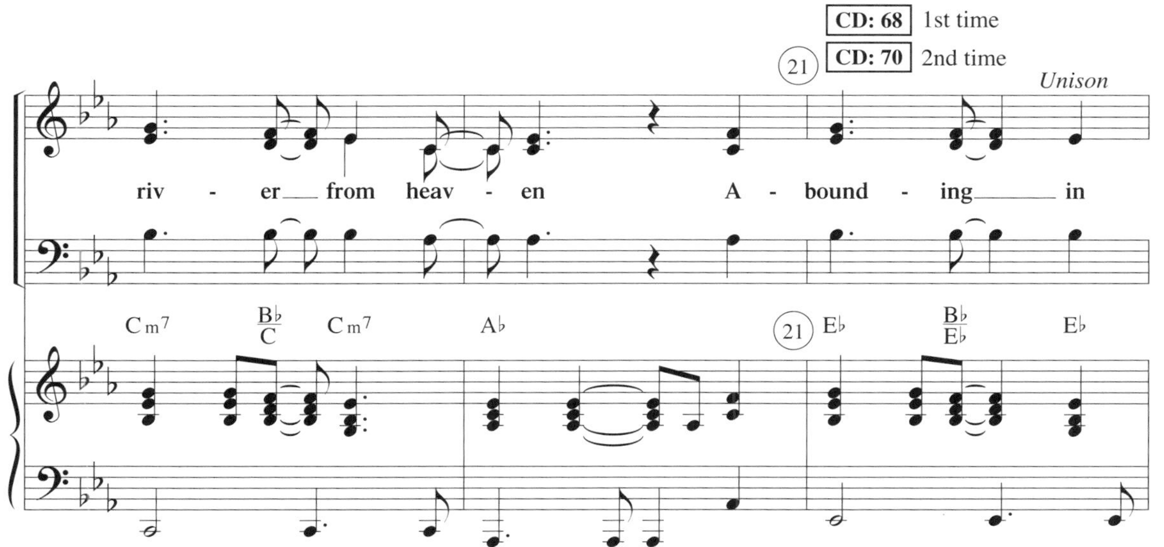
CD: 68 1st time
CD: 70 2nd time
21
Unison
riv - er from heav - en A - bound - ing in
Cm7
B♭/C
Cm7
A♭
21
E♭
B♭/E♭
E♭

love to my soul.
All
B♭ B♭sus B♭ A♭
25 Half-time feel
bless - ing and hon - or are His,
25
A♭
E♭/G
Fm
29
All glo - ry and pow - er are
Fm
E♭2/G
29 A♭
E♭/G

33
His.
Let all wis - dom and
Fm
E♭2
G
33
A♭
strength be the Lord's in this place. Let all
E♭
G
A♭
E♭
G
CD: 69 1st time
37
CD: 71 2nd time
1
Divisi
glo - ry be giv - en to Him.
37
Fm7
D♭M7
1
B♭sus

(to pg. 108, meas. 9)
Unison
2
Divisi
Unison
f
There is
Him.
There is
f
(to pg. 108, meas. 9)
B♭ A♭ B♭
2
B♭sus
B♭ C
43
joy in the Lord, there is love in His Spir-
43
F C Csus C Dm7
f
47
-it, There is hope in the know - ledge of
B♭
47
F C Csus C

Divisi
51
Him.
There's a foun - tain I know;
B♭
C
F
C/F
F
ev - 'ry time I am near it My
C
C sus
C
D m7
C/D
D m7
B♭
55
CD: 72
Unison
heart o - ver - flows to the Lord.
F
C/F
F
C
C sus
C
B♭

Divisi
59
There is joy, there is
Divisi
B♭
C
F
love, There is hope in the
Unison
63
Dm7
F/B♭
CD: 73
know - ledge of Him.
C
Csus
B♭/D
C/E

68
Divisi
There is joy in the Lord, there is
Divisi
C
E
G
D
Dsus
D
love in His Spir - it, There is
Em7
C
72
hope in the know - ledge of Him.
G
D
Dsus
D
C

76
Unison
There's a foun - tain that flows,
Like a
Unison
C D G D/G G D Dsus D
riv - er from heav - en
80 Divisi
A - bound - ing in
Divisi
Em7 D/E Em7 C G D/G G
CD: 74
love to my soul.
D Dsus D C

84
Joy in the Lord, love in His Spir-
84
G Am/G G D Em7 Am/E Em7
88
- it, Hope in the know - ledge of
C 88 G Am/G G D Dsus D
1
Him, of Him.
C
1

2
93
ff
Him.
There's joy in the Lord!
ff
2
C
93
ff

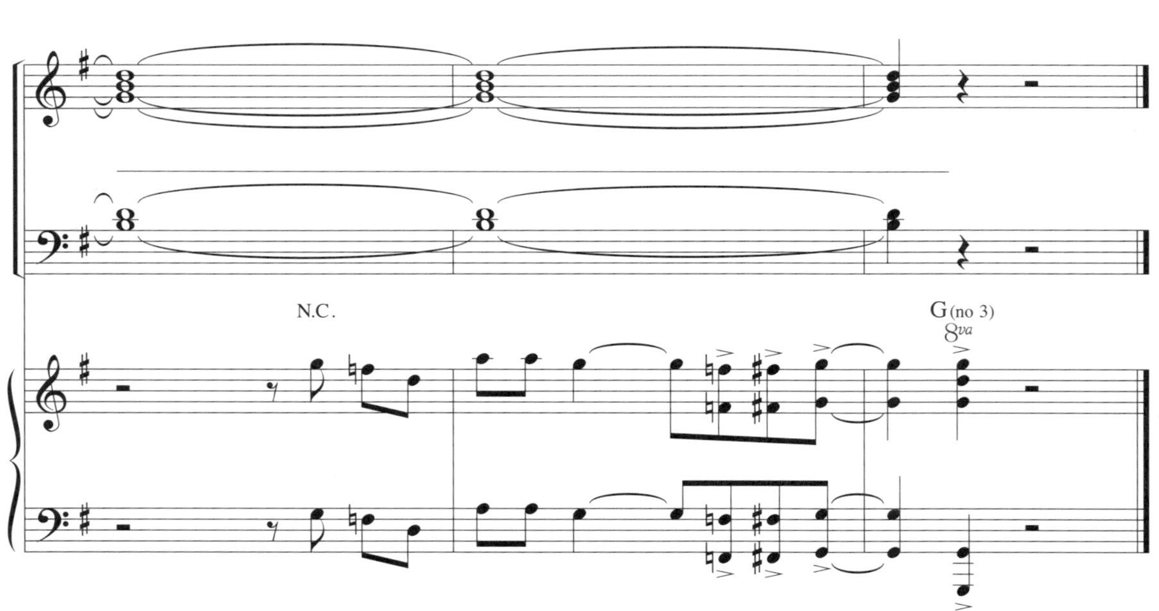
N.C.
G(no 3)
8va

I Need You More

with

I Need Thee Every Hour

Words and Music by
LINDELL COOLEY
and BRUCE HAYNES
Arranged by Marty Parks

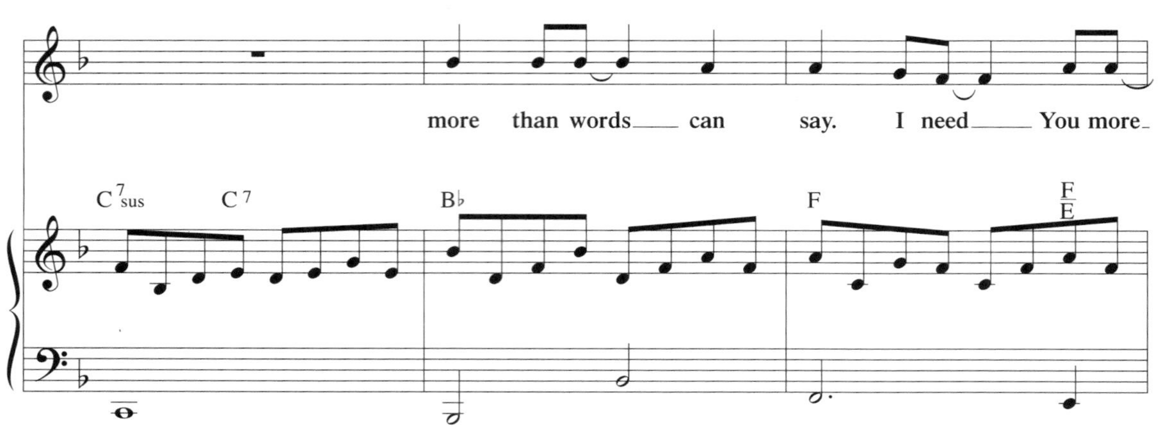
more than words can say. I need You more
C7sus
C7
B♭
F
F/E

13
than ev - er be -
Dm2
Gm

17
CD: 76
fore, I need You, Lord, I need You,
G°7
D♭°7
F/C
Csus
C7

Choir
Unison mp
21
Lord.
More than the air I breathe,
Unison mp
F2
F2/A
B♭2
More than the song I sing;
More than the next
B♭2
C sus
D m7
25
heart - beat,
Divisi
More than an - y -
Divisi
B♭2
G m
C6

Unison
29
Divisi
And, Lord, as time goes by
thing.
Lord, as time goes by
I'll be by
Unison
Divisi
F
F2/A
29
B♭2
C
Solo
33
Your side,
'Cause I nev - er want to go
C
Dm
33
Gm
CD: 77
back to my old life.
Choir
I need You more,
F/A
C7sus
B♭/C

37
more than yes - ter - day;
37 F2
F/G Gm
41
I need You more,
Gm Gm6/D 41 Csus C7
45
more than words can say. I need You more
Gm7 C7 C6 F F/E 45 Dm

than ev - er be - fore, I need You, Lord,
Dm
F/G
Gm
F/D
B♭m6/G
49
I need You, Lord.
F2
B♭/C
C7
F
CD: 78
55
*"I Need Thee Every Hour"
Unison mf I need
B♭M7
F
cresc.
B♭2
B♭/C
F
mf

59

Thee ev - 'ry hour, Most gra -

B♭M7 F E♭/F F7 59 B♭M7

mf 63

- cious Lord; No ten -

Gm7 B♭/C F F2 63 Gm Gm7

67

- der voice like Thine mel. Can peace

C7 C7/E F Dm Dm7 67 G6 F/G

CD: 79

71 *Solo, 2nd time only*

more,

af - ford.

I need

Divisi

G G9 G6 G7 C C4/2 C C7 C13 71 F

more than yes - ter-day; I need You more,

Thee; O I need Thee!

F B♭/F F Gm2 Gm

75
more than words can
Ev - 'ry hour I need
C7sus
C7 B♭/C F/C C7 Gm/F
say. I need You more
79
than
Thee! O bless me now, my
F F/A
B♭M7
B♭ B♭6 B♭M7 B♭

83
ev - er be - fore, I need You, Lord,
Sav - ior; I come
F F2 B♭ G°7 83 F2/C
CD: 80 1st time
CD: 81 2nd time
1
(to pg. 126, meas. 71)
mf
I need You, I need You
to Thee! I
F2/C C7 1 F B♭/C C13
(to pg. 126, meas. 71)

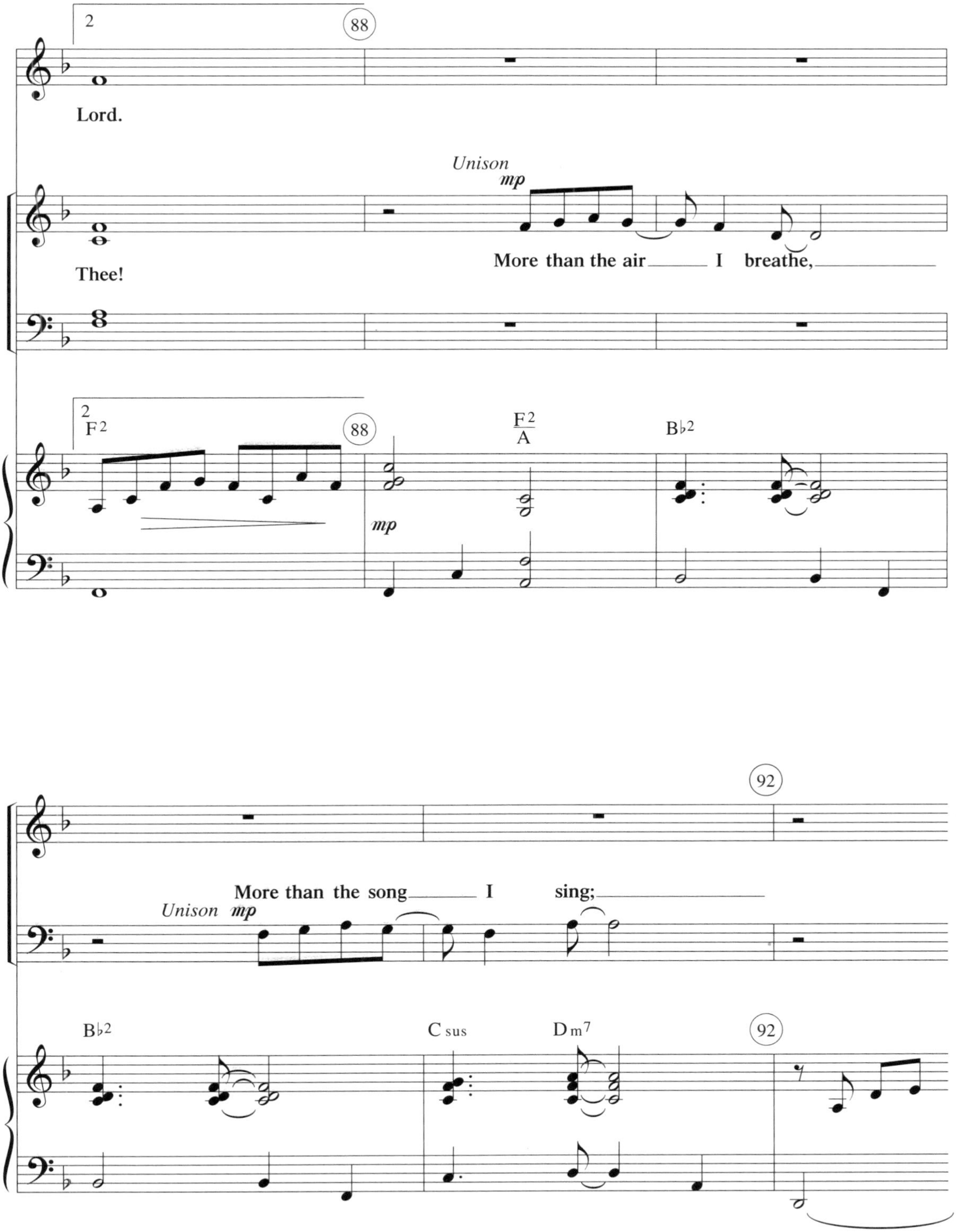

2

88

Lord.

Unison

mp

Thee!

More than the air I breathe,

2

F2

88

F2/A

B♭2

mp

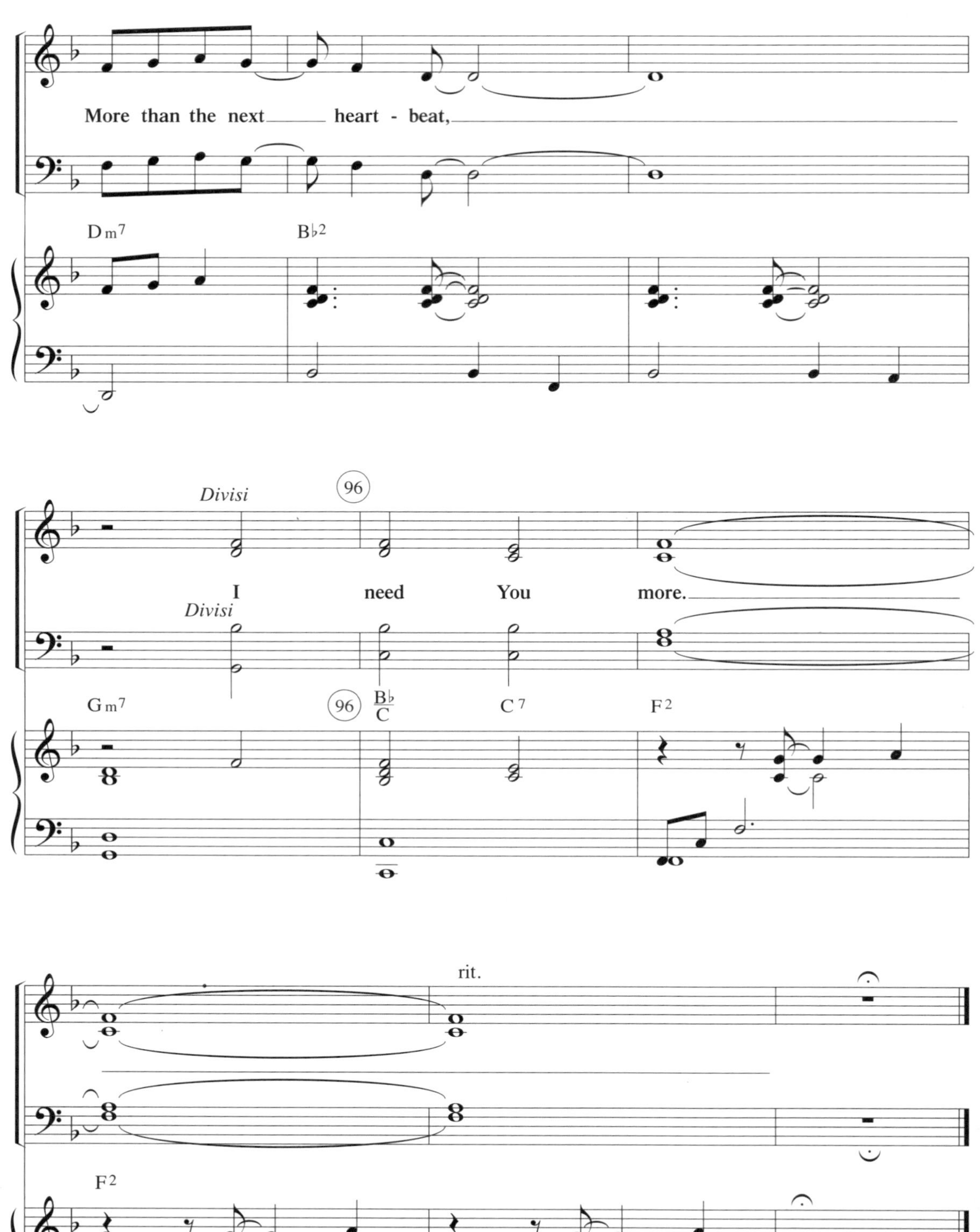
More than the next heart - beat,
Dm7
B♭2
Divisi
96
I need You more.
Divisi
Gm7
96
B♭/C
C7
F2
rit.
F2
rit.

All Praise Rising

Words and Music by
LUKE GARRETT
Arranged by Richard Kingsmore

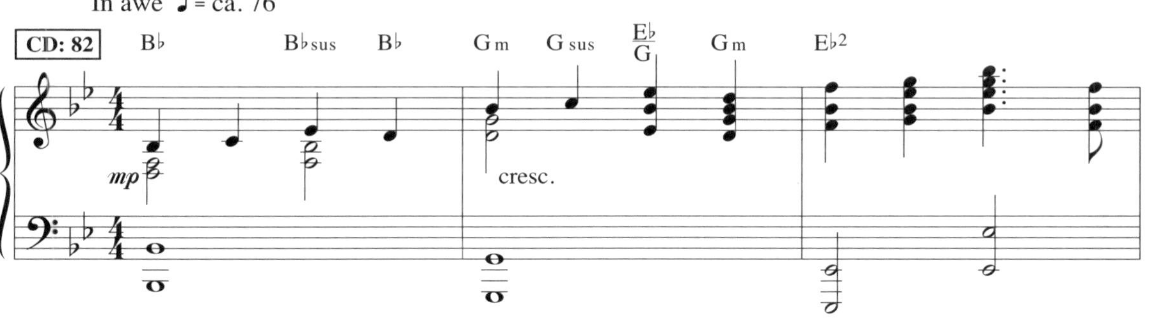

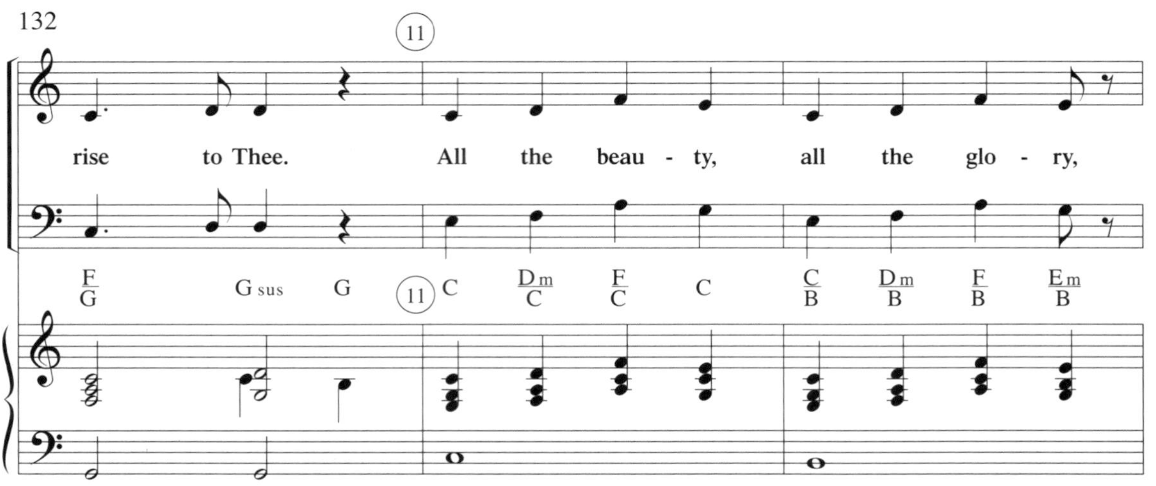
11
rise to Thee. All the beau - ty, all the glo - ry,
F/G Gsus G C Dm/C F/C C C/B Dm/B F/B Em/B
11

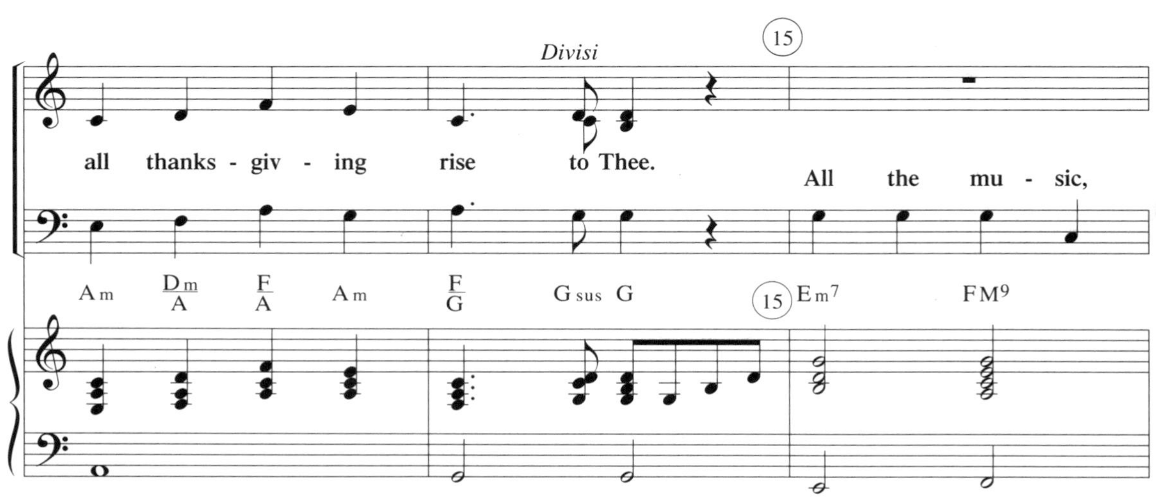
Divisi
15
all thanks - giv - ing rise to Thee.
All the mu - sic,
Am Dm/A F/A Am F/G Gsus G Em7 FM9
15

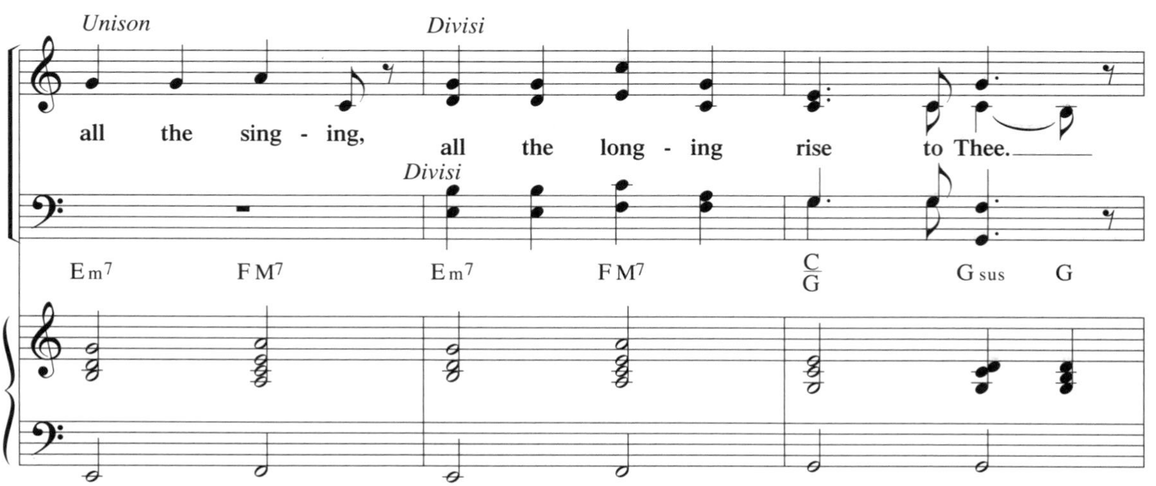
Unison
Divisi
all the sing - ing, all the long - ing rise to Thee.
Divisi
Em7 FM7 Em7 FM7 C/G Gsus G

19
Unison
In the sor - row, and the laugh - ter, all praise ris - ing,
Unison
C
Dm/C
F/C
C
C/B
Dm/B
F/B
Em/B
Am
G
F
C/E
Divisi
24
cresc. poco a poco
It will
rise to Thee.
And it will rise,
Dm7
Dm7/G
C
C/B
rise,
will rise,
will rise to Thee.
It will
Am7
F/A
C/G
F
C/E
C/D
Gsus/D
F6/G

28
rise,
it will
rise
it will rise,
will
C
C
B
Am7
F6
A
C
G

rise,
will
rise
to
Thee.
FM7
C
E
G sus
F
G
C

33
CD: 84
Male solo
mf
If there be
FM7
Em7
Dm7
B♭M7
Am7
F
G
F6
G
mp

37

an - y peace, an - y love; If there be an - y joy, let them

Unison **mf**

Tenors only Let them **mf**

37 FM7 Em7 Dm7 B♭M7 Am7

mf

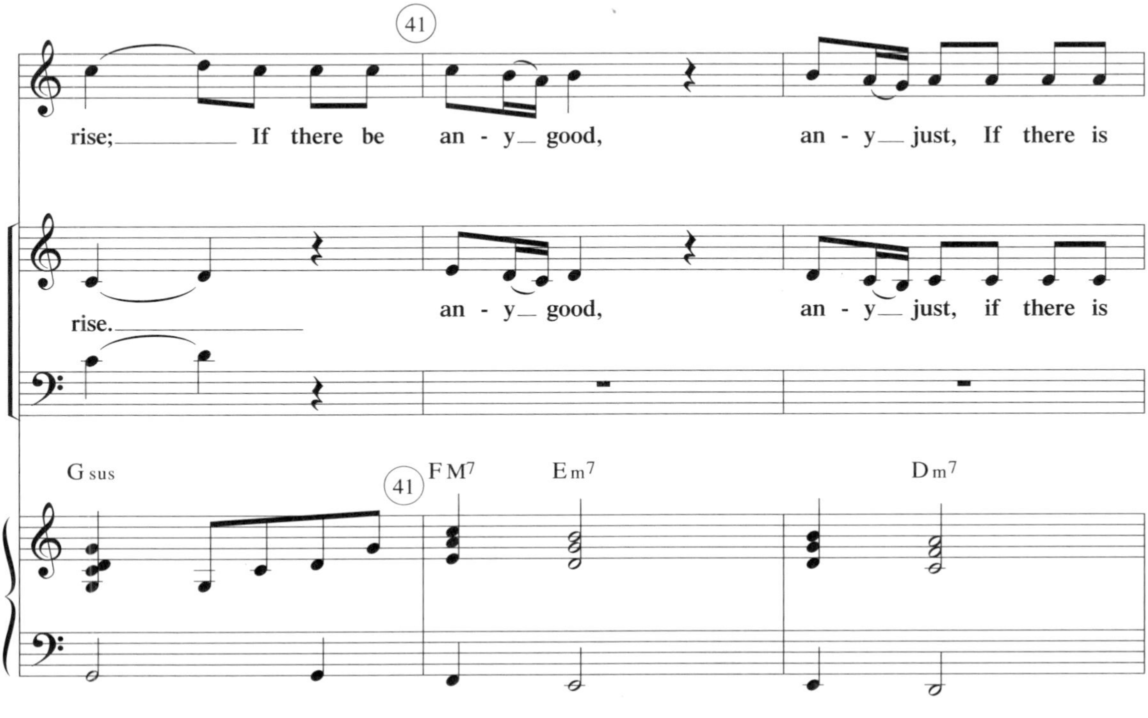

41

rise; If there be an - y good, an - y just, If there is

rise. an - y good, an - y just, if there is

G sus 41 FM7 Em7 Dm7

45

an - y _ grace, Let it rise; ___ If there is an - y _ breath,

Divisi

an - y grace, Let it rise; ___ an - y _ breath,

B♭M9 A m7 G sus 45 F M7 E m7

CD: 85

f

an - y sound, If there is an - y _ life, Let it rise; ___ Let it

an - y sound, An - y life, *Add bass* Let it rise; ___

E m7 D m7 B♭M7 A m7 G sus D m/G A m/G

49

rise. Ev - 'ry hon - or

f

All praise ris - ing, all re - joic - ing, Ev - 'ry hon - or

f

49 C Dm/C F/C C C/B Gsus/B F/B Em/B Am Dm/A Dm7 C/E

f

rise to Thee. 53 All the beau - ty, all the glo - ry,

rise to Thee. All the beau - ty, all the glo - ry,

F Gsus G 53 C Dm/C F/C C C/B Gsus/B F/B Em/B

57

all thanks - giv - ing rise to Thee.

mf

all thanks - giv - ing rise to Thee. All the mu - sic,

Am Dm/A Dm7 C/E F Gsus G 57 Em7 FM7

mf

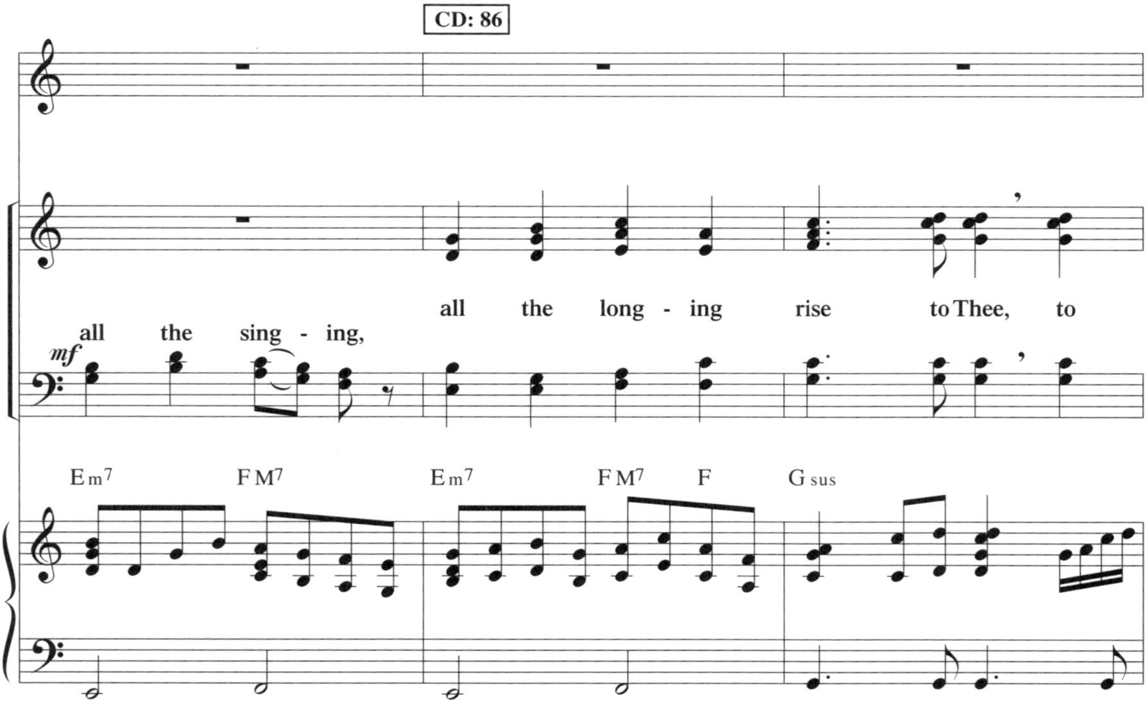

CD: 86

all the long - ing rise to Thee, to

mf all the sing - ing,

Em7 FM7 Em7 FM7 F Gsus

f rit.
62
a tempo
O let it rise,
Thee.
In the sorrow
Ab sus
Bbm/Ab
Gb/Ab
62
Db
Ebm/Db
Gb/Db
Db
rit.
f a tempo
CD: 87
in laughter, all praise rising,
and the laughter, all praise rising,
Db/C
Ab sus/C
Gb/C
Fm/C
Bbm
Ebm/Bb
Ebm7
Db/F

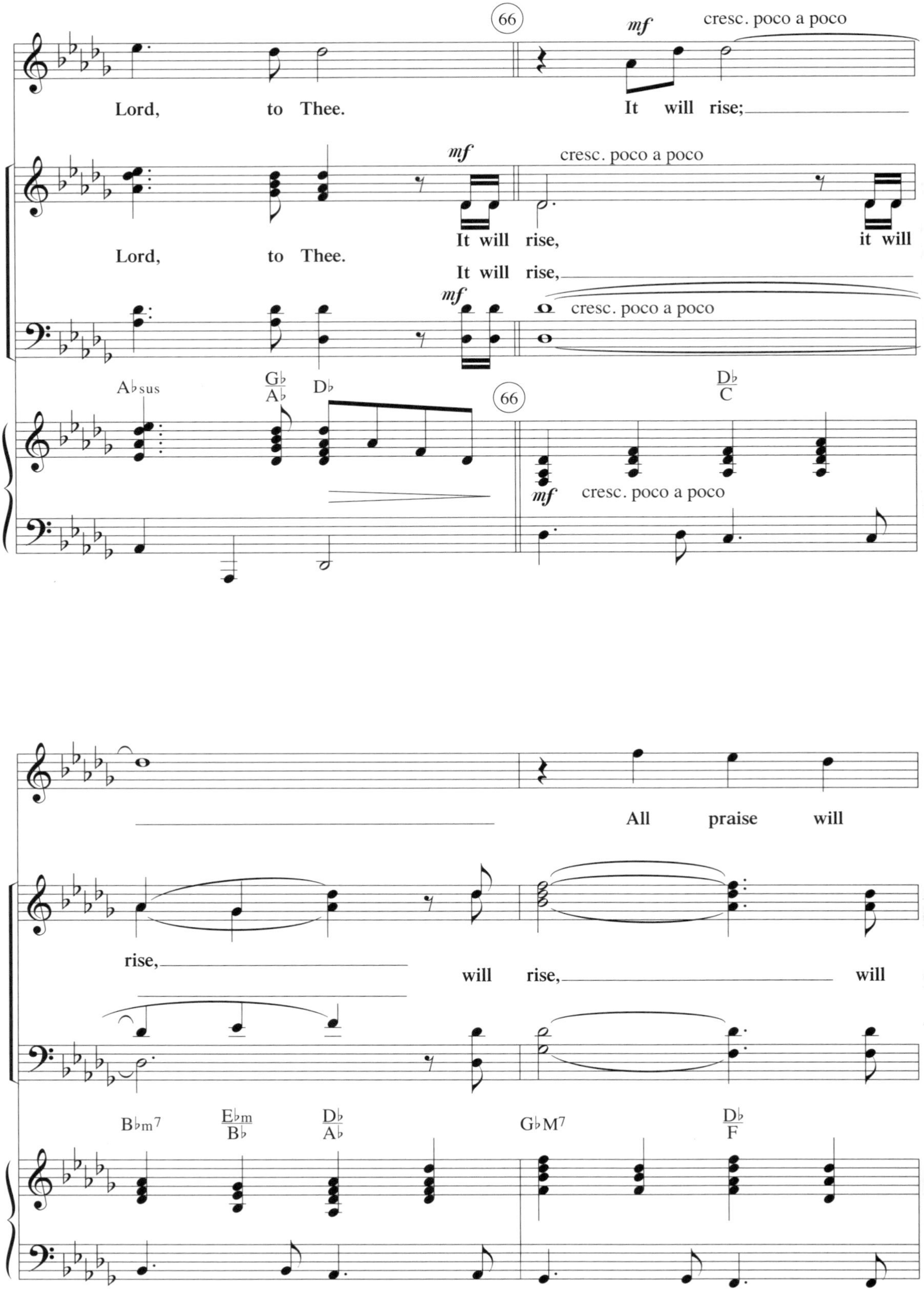

66

mf cresc. poco a poco

Lord, to Thee. It will rise;

mf cresc. poco a poco

It will rise, it will

Lord, to Thee.

It will rise,

mf cresc. poco a poco

A♭sus G♭/A♭ D♭ 66 D♭/C

mf cresc. poco a poco

All praise will

rise, will rise, will

B♭m7 E♭m/B♭ D♭/A♭ G♭M7 D♭/F

70

rise to Thee. It will rise; ____

rise to Thee. It will rise, it will

E♭m7 A♭sus 70 D♭ D♭/C

____ It will rise, will rise to

rise, ____ will rise, ____ will rise to

B♭m D♭/A♭ G♭M9 D♭/F E♭m7/A♭

Thee.
Thee.
It will
D♭
E♭m/D♭
G♭/D♭
D♭

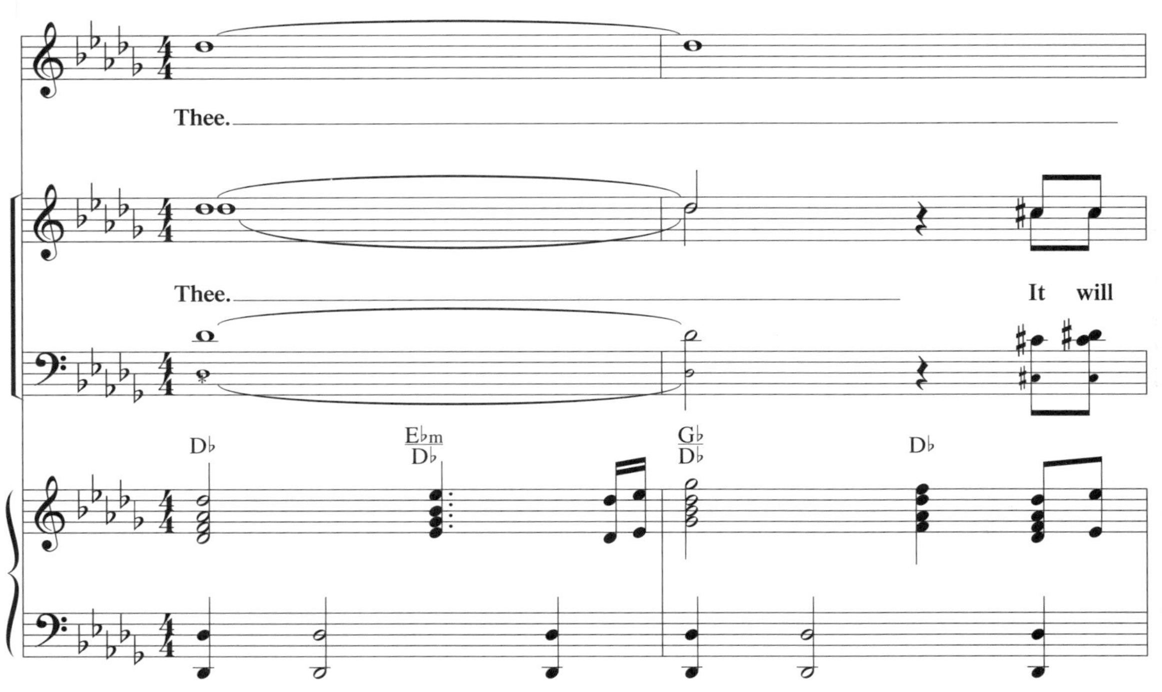

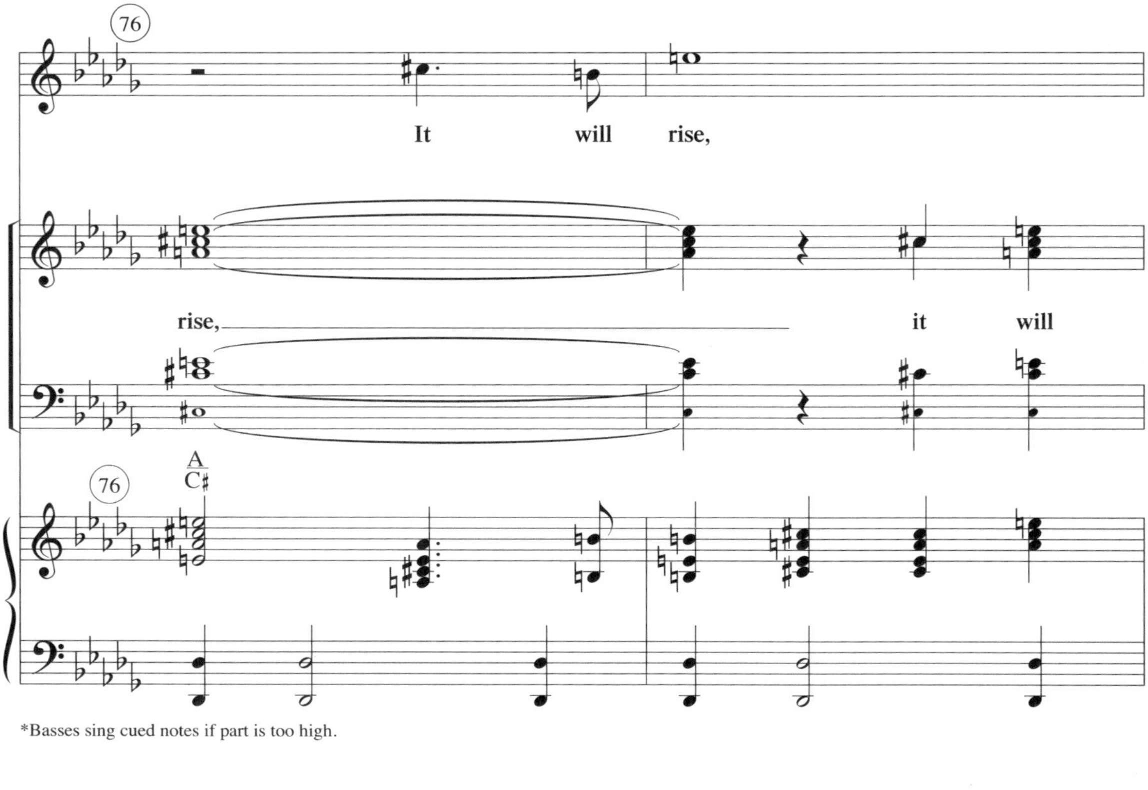

76
It will rise,
rise,
it will
A/C♯
76

*Basses sing cued notes if part is too high.

it will rise,

ff

rise, it will

ff

F♯m6/C♯

F♯m/C♯ N.C.

ff

(♭) (♭)

80

ff rit.

(6)

it will rise.

rise.

80

D♭

rit.

8vb